Marriage Maintenance

Getting Back on the Road to Romance

TAM AND BRYAN LITTLE

For permission request for excerpts contact publisher at contact@tamlittle. com. Books may be purchased in bulk for promotional, educational, and business use.

ISBN 978-0-578-68731-5

Library of Congress Control Number: 2020924229

Scripture quotations, unless otherwise indicated, are taken from the Holy Bible, New All International Version®, NIV®. Copyright ©1973, 1978, 1984, 2011 by Biblica, Inc.™ Used by permission of Zondervan. All rights reserved worldwide. www.zondervan.com. The "NIV" and "New International Version" are trademarks registered in the United States Patent and Trademark Office by Biblica, Inc.™

Scripture quotations marked (NLT) are taken from the Holy Bible, New Living Translation, copyright ©1996, 2004, 2015 by Tyndale House Foundation. Used by permission of Tyndale House Publishers, a Division of Tyndale House Ministries, Carol Stream, Illinois 60188. All rights reserved.

Publisher: VirtualBay Publishing

For more information: contact@tamlittle.com

Cover design: Tam Little Cover image: Olga Apostolova

This book is a resource intended for marriage enrichment purposes. It should not be used to replace the specialized training and professional judgment of health care, mental health, or licensed marriage professionals. The authors do not assume liability for loss or damage caused by errors or omissions. If you discover that exercises contained in this book raise issues that cannot be easily resolved, please always consult a licensed professional before making any decision regarding treatment of yourself or others.

We hope that you enjoy this book from Tam and Bryan Little. Our goal is to provide you with transformational, engaging, and thought-provoking books that meet the needs of marriages and families for generations to come.

Website: www.tamlittle.com

We dedicate this book to

Pastor David C. Rourk and First Lady Ruth Rourk
&
Deacon George and Deaconess Archie Bruce

*You showed us the meaning of what sacrificial and lasting love looks like.
We live by your example and our desire is to be a light, showing the world
marriage can be a thing of beauty, exemplifying God's love.
May the love you have for one another live on as examples for
generations to come.*

*Love,
Bryan and Tam*

Contents

A Personal Note from Bryan & Tam

*T*hank you for picking up your copy of *Marriage Maintenance: Getting Back on the Road to Romance!* We are so glad you decided to hop in and join us on the journey! This will be an adventure for couples and is sure to be quite the ride. It definitely has been for us these past 21 years! Whether you have been married two days, two weeks, or twenty years, there is always something new to learn about your spouse. As we stop along different points throughout this journey, you are sure to find valuable nuggets along the way.

If you are single, thank you for picking up a copy of *Marriage Maintenance* as well. We don't want to leave you out. We hope that by providing you with an intimate look at marriage, this book will provide you with the tools you'll need to make wise and well informed decisions when choosing a spouse. Hindsight is always 20/20, so use this book as a guide to gain foresight for your current or future relationship.

Before we start our engines, we'd like to ask you a few questions. Have you been married for several years and would like to infuse a bit of newness in your marriage? Does romance feel like a distant memory? Are there unexpected detours that have prevented you from having the times of closeness you need or desire, and is self-care or couple care the last thing you think about but is still important to you? If you answered, "That's us," "Used to be us," or "Could be us," to any of these questions, we are with you. One day, we had to take a hard look at our marriage, face these questions, and work together to move our marriage to a place where we both felt heard and valued. If romance seems like a distant memory due to work, family, and business obligations, our desire is that after reading this love manual, you will recommit to making romance, time alone, and your relationship a top priority. If you are doing extremely well in this area, don't stop reading just yet, there's always something new and exciting you can uncover about your spouse. They are just waiting to be rediscovered!

Understanding that there are many variables that may cause a relationship that once sizzled to fizzle, we will take you on a journey down memory lane and over a few scenic landscapes to give you an opportunity to remember the little things that made you fall in love. We will also give you a moment to pull over and take some time to rest, so that you'll have the energy to take care of your spouse and to be taken care of during times when you both need it the most. By the end of the journey, we will have guided you to lover's lane, where we have a few surprises and exercises you can both do together that will definitely spice things up and will draw you even closer together.

However, before moving ahead, we do need to provide you with a disclaimer: engaging in a lifestyle of continual connections is not always easy. We don't want to provide you with a few quick-fix ideas like those you'd read while standing in line at your local grocery store. We have all seen the catchy headlines: "30

Surefire Ways to Keep the Romance Alive," and "40 Ways to Have the Best Night Ever." Those attention-grabbing headlines are creative and offer a great deal of spontaneity, but those great ideas can soon fizzle out once "life happens." An unexpected car repair, growing debt, mounting bills, fatigue, and long work hours can quickly divert your attention from your relationship. We found after reading many of those "how-to" lists; there are no quick fixes when it comes to developing a strong relationship with the one you love; there's only the commitment of time and intentionality.

Writing together during the Covid-19 pandemic gave us an opportunity to refocus on the things that were most important to us; our family and our relationship. We underestimated the value of intimacy and connecting when Covid-19 took the world by surprise. Romance, dating, and how we spend time together as couples looks very different during a pandemic! Wearing face masks, donning gloves, and practicing social distancing in places where we once enjoyed frequenting has become our new reality. Now, more than ever is the time to begin dating again and prioritizing our relationships.

We understand life happens; children must be reared, bills have to be paid, roles in our businesses and jobs must be fulfilled. However, one day, the children will grow up, jobs will change, and the bill we worried about will eventually be paid. These life occurrences will fluctuate throughout your marriage, but the love and commitment you have for your spouse does not have to. Even if you haven't traveled the road to romance for a while, know there are ultimately "no rules" to romance and how you choose to spend quality time together. Brela Delahoussaye, the founder of Romance Me, explains that romance is simply, "**R**ecognizing

Opportunities and **M**aintaining **A**ffection **N**ecessary for **C**reating **E**verlasting love." If you and your spouse are looking for opportunities to create lasting love, you are sure to find it. Meaningful connections do not have to fade into the sunset after ten, twenty, or even thirty years of marriage. Consistently taking the time and the opportunity daily to recognize your spouse is your friend, life partner, and ally makes for a richer marriage.

YOU ARE RICHER THAN THE 1%

There's a common theme relegated to rich and successful individuals found in wealth-building articles in publications such as *Kiplinger's*, *Forbes*, and *Bloomberg Businessweek*. These periodicals tout:

Successful People:
- See the possibilities
- Take calculated risks
- Invest in themselves
- Press past obstacles and challenging experiences

These habits are not just exclusively for the wealthy or the 1%. They're also important in our marriage and relationships. Financial security is beneficial; however, there are more important things in life. Some may disagree, but ask the widow or widower who has lost the love of their life. They would gladly give all of their earthly possessions to be with their spouse again. Being rich in love, having a home filled with peace, and being loved in return are invaluable commodities countless people long for. So, how does that compare with successful marriages on this journey?

Successful Marriages:
- See the possibilities of sharing a life together years after they say "I do"
- Take risks to love, trust, and forgive again after misunderstandings
- Purposely invest time in their relationship to ensure it thrives

- Press past life obstacles and work through challenging marital seasons

Most importantly, successful marriages work toward being optimistic about their future and life together. We believe you are that successful couple (or person in a future committed relationship) because you have invested in yourselves by picking up a copy of *Marriage Maintenance*, and we are so glad that you did.

Chapter One

Love Manuals and Mechanics

As you go on this journey together, we want you to think of us as your love mechanics and this book as your love manual. After 21 years of marriage, we've had wonderful opportunities to coach, mentor, and facilitate counseling sessions with couples from all walks of life; from those dating considering engagement, to couples who have been married for many years that simply just want a couple tune-up session with us from time to time. As certified marriage mentors through Prepare and Enrich, the leading marital and premarital counseling education program, our goal is to encourage couples to build strong and healthy relationships by actively listening to one another through open and honest communication.

Much like your personal mechanic, this resource is available for you when you need it. We designed this book to be engaging and have provided you with several exciting tidbits and activities to help turbo-boost your relationship. We chose to explore how marriage is very similar to going on an exciting journey, which you will see throughout each chapter. While these road trips may be exciting, the vehicle you are both traveling in may require maintenance from time to time to ensure you reach your desired destination. We want to make sure you have an exciting, successful, and romantic journey, so we will provide you with a few necessities for your journey. A roadmap will also be provided to help you navigate any detours or delays you may experience along the way.

Like many of you, we've experienced firsthand what happens when you don't check the gas gauge, change the oil regularly, or go in for those time-consuming annual inspections. When we failed to do those "little things" along the way, we found ourselves out of gas along a dark, dusty road next to a cemetery (true story). Early in our marriage, we were forced to purchase a costly new transmission because we failed to address a long-standing issue, and on top of that, we had to bail our car out of car jail because we were towed for an expired registration sticker.

We don't anticipate anyone having to bail their car out of car jail! However, we do understand, from experience, that failing to take care of your marriage (and vehicle) consistently can become quite costly mentally, emotionally, and, in some cases, financially. It does not matter if you have been married 5 days, 5 months, or 50 years. All marriages will require maintenance from time to time. It's the little things that keep the marriage running optimally when both spouses feel valued and their love tanks are being filled.

As we have promised to be with you on this journey, we ask that you to make a promise to yourselves to complete all of the activities included. Each chapter will consist of activities that you and your spouse can do together, using progressively thought-provoking questions. The goal is to gain greater clarity of your spouse's perspective, to create an open dialogue, and bring you closer together. On a few occasions, you may have to prayerfully approach and discuss sensitive topics that may not have been addressed for some time. During those times, keep an open mind and always remember you are on the same team.

This book is a safe space. If there are areas you think you would like to lead up to, feel free to circle back to them. We encourage you to complete all of the activities because many exercises lead into others. Each exercise is a practice opportunity, not a test, so they should be enjoyed. If an activity seems easy, write your answers anyway rather than thinking them through. Thinking is a quick way to go over the exercises, but writing them in your own words will allow you to engage with your spouse and connect on a deeper level.

If you find you are completing the tasks with flying colors, celebrate your strengths and feel free to use this book as a guide to help strengthen other couples in your sphere of influence. We want you to be successful, so as you advance through the book, take advantage of your R & R (Rest and Reading times) in each section, and thoughtfully focus on your relationship. As you read through each chapter, commit to being present and intentional. Discovering one another again is a part of the journey, and because of this, there are no "right" answers, shortcuts, or quick fixes. Your relationship is like a fingerprint, unique, and like no one else's, so that makes it valuable.

The following five steps will help you successfully navigate your journey:

1. Agree to Focus on Each Other and Your Marriage

Agree that this will be a time set apart exclusively for you and your spouse. Remember, this is not a school assignment; instead, it is designed to revive, refuel, and refocus your relationship. We recommend that you carve out time <u>one day during the week</u> to discuss each chapter›s activities, bonus homework challenges, and practice what you've learned throughout the week.

We understand; we all seem to be in a perpetual state of feeling like there are never enough hours in a day. As much as we'd like to have time part for us like Moses standing in front of the Red Sea, it doesn't always have to take a miracle to set aside a few minutes each day for the one we love. It takes intentionality to carve out time for your spouse, the person you fell in love with before the kids, bills, and life challenges.

2. Anticipate Your Time Together

Once you select a specific time in advance, you're more apt to do what you look forward to. Send a love note, a sweet little text, or even whisper in their ear in passing, telling your spouse that you're looking forward to being alone with them. Don't be shy. Flirt a little!

3. Don't Forget to Reward Yourselves

You deserve recognition for your completion and commitment after each section, so celebrate! Little wins are always sweeter when you win them together. Take turns deciding how to celebrate your completion successes. Focus on your favorite things and remember, it does not have to be expensive. Go out for a fancy coffee, get in the car and go for a drive, or go to your favorite eatery! Be creative!

4. Plan for Interruptions

We all have good intentions to complete things that will help us grow. Life happens, unexpected problems arise, and you may have to change your plans. If this occurs, reschedule the new time and stick to it. Also, if you can, get a sitter. Let family and friends know that you and your spouse are spending a couple of hours together to build on your marriage over the next few weeks. Don't have a sitter? Press on, put the kids to bed a little bit earlier, hang in there, and protect the time you have together.

5. Use Caution and Couple Codes

Please be aware: whenever you desire to invest in yourself and your marriage, there will always be opposing forces. The good news is you are more than capable of heading them off. Do not use this time together to deal with problems. Even though you may discuss past issues, make sure that you stay positive and focused on the future. Ask yourselves each week, "What have we learned?" or "What will we re-establish this week?" If you find yourself veering towards detours, stop, redirect, and refocus.

Establish your couple code words in case you need to take a break and revisit an issue. We have several codes we use publicly and privately to communicate with one another. Codes can range from, "We probably should stop here", "Is everything okay?", "I'm not so sure about that person," to the infamous,

"Don't pick up that chicken with your hands in front of guests," code. It can be a subtle look, simple hand gesture, or even an unassuming word. It's up to you, but you'll need to establish a few Couple Code signals to help you navigate smoothly through certain sections. Do what works best for you to get yourselves back on track and headed in the right direction.

OUR COMMITMENT TO YOUR JOURNEY

We are committed to your success, but we'd like to affirm that you are committed to the journey as well. Therefore, we have included our signatures as a sign of our commitment to you; indicating that we have prayed for God to bless you and your marriage.

Your Name

Spouse's Name

Before you set out on your new adventure, we'd like to say a short prayer for you so that your time together will be blessed and productive.

Dear Lord,

Thank you for each spouse reading today, those who desire a spouse, and ones desiring to reconnect with their spouse. We pray that you would bless their lives and reveal to them the great love you have for them. We believe you bring spouses together and since you brought them together, we know that you have the power and ability to help them build on the love they have for one another. Please give them the strength they need to be transparent, understanding, and forgiving during challenging times. If there are sensitive areas that need to be discussed, help them to resolve each issue graciously full of love and humility. If there are things they need to let go of in their hearts due to past hurts or misunderstandings, give them the wisdom to address them and leave behind issues they have committed to resolve. Give them new eyes to see their spouse in a new way and a heart full of anticipation for the possibilities and future that is before them. Father, for those seeking a spouse show them what true love is in your Word, so that when the time comes they will be able to identify it and will accept nothing less. We thank you for a new beginning.

In Jesus' name we pray,

Amen

LOVER'S LANE: LOVE MADE ME DO IT

Before we delve any deeper, let's park and take a few moments to reminisce about where it all began. Do you remember falling in love? What it felt like? Do you remember feeling butterflies in your stomach? Who can forget the kisses that made your heart melt, how your heart raced when you saw your love from afar, or that tingling sensation when you touched?

Many Millennials and Gen Z's may not ever experience the times when older generations would stay on the phone talking to one another (on a landline) until the wee hours in the morning. Neither wanted to hang up, so you both sat there until you could only hear the shallowness of your love's breathing and were suddenly awakened by a blaring dial tone. We've all experienced the newness of love and times when we could not get enough of each other.

The song *Ain't No Mountain High Enough* by Marvin Gaye and Tammi Terrell, is the anthem for the lengths couples will go for love. The song touts of a lover's willingness to scale a mountain, trek miles through barren lands, and swim through treacherous waters just to be with the one they love. So what causes us to feel that way? Scientific studies found that during the early stages of love, when we are willing to scale mountains while walking on cloud nine, we were actually walking in a plume of dopamine. This love and bonding hormone, along with its close relatives: oxytocin, testosterone, serotonin and a host of other happy hormones, actually flooded our brains, making us feel pleasure, passion, and love for our intended. These hormones are also responsible for helping us create strong bonds of intimacy and the wonderful news is, they are always ready to be activated and revved up.

It doesn't matter how long you've been married; you can always experience those giddy feelings of love, and one way to rev them up again is to simply begin by remembering the love you have for your spouse and how you fell in love. In this first section, while you're still on Lover's Lane, we want you to take a trip down memory lane and remember when you fell in love. Feelings fluctuate based on the season of marriage you're in, but mature love endures. This maturation of love allows us to develop into oneness and sustains us for years to come.

YOUR STORY

Take a few moments to remember the beauty of the first time you fell in love. Answer the questions below and share these little tidbits of love with your spouse.

Visualize and think about the first time you met your spouse.

1. How did your friendship develop?

_____

2. What did you notice about your spouse when you first met?

_____

3. When did you know your spouse was "the one?"

_____

4. What personality characteristics caught your attention?

_____

5. What do you love most about your spouse now?

_____

_____

_____

_____

_____

6. What is the glue that keeps you together?

_____

_____

_____

_____

HOMEWORK CHALLENGE #1

Notes of Love

Do you want to add a bit more spice to this exercise? If so, write your spouse a little love note reminding them why you love them and how important they are to you. You determine how spicy you want it to be. The goal is to carve out a quiet time this week to share those tidbits of love with your spouse and present it to them.

Did you complete the questions and homework challenge?

If you did, then you and your spouse should reward yourselves! Do something spontaneous that you've wanted to do for some time but haven't. Remember, it does not have to cost a great deal of money to have meaningful time together!

We commit to rewarding ourselves this week by:

Did you finish the questions? Write your love note? Great job! Then move on to the next chapter. We hope you and your spouse are prepared to get revved up for the next section; but first you'll need your keys.

Chapter Two

Do You Have Your Keys?

ave you ever lost your keys? The very thought of losing one's keys can strike fear into even the bravest of hearts. Why? Because at that moment, we realize without those two-inch pieces of metal, we no longer have access to some of our most precious possessions. Whether your home, car, or safety deposit box, keys give access into a desired door, room, or location and it can be costly if they aren't found. As we set out on the next portion of our journey, we'll need to make sure you have two vital necessities to get started and stay on your lifelong journey of closeness, romance, and emotional connection with your spouse.

Like cars, all marriages have different styles and features, but the one thing they all have in common is the need to be in a progressive state of motion to reach their desired destination. So, what do we need to get there? Keys and fuel. Much like the key and gas you need for your car, communication and trust are vital in marriage; and without them, your marriage is either stalled or stranded on the side of the road.

It can be challenging to have a romantic and intimate relationship if you and your spouse are not communicating well. How we speak and respond to one another is an essential key to our relationships. Your words, like the right keys, grant you access to your spouse's heart, permitting you to unlock priceless treasures of friendship and love. On their wedding day, all newlywed couples receive "marital keys" and must understand the power they hold in their hands. On that day, bearers of those keys are granted access to the heart of their spouse. However, if you abuse or misuse this power, you may discover one day that the locks have changed on your spouse's heart, leaving you in the cold and forcing you to earn a new set of keys to gain access again.

Communication between two people of the opposite sex with different backgrounds, upbringings, and values can be quite complex. It takes a lifetime to truly master the art of discovering the different facets of your spouse. You may not always want to read the car manual in your glove compartment, but at some point you'll want to know how to pair your Bluetooth to your phone or find that cleverly hidden latch to open the gas tank. Your spouse may be very much like a manual; a bit complex at times but you will always find the answers you need when you take the time to look a little closer. You will always be a student of your spouse and them of you. The willingness to learn how to communicate and adapt to your spouse is an invaluable lifelong skill you will always be required to hone if you desire a good marriage. You'll discover, if you haven't already, that both you and your spouse throughout your marriage will change, grow, and mature at different times. Anticipate those changes because you'll always have to know which key to use. Initially, you may stumble a bit, but over time, like finding the right key in the dark, you will eventually find it.

COMMUNICATION KEYS

It is not uncommon for a young married couple to ask an older seasoned couple, "What's the secret to a good marriage?" Although we continue to hear the number one secret to all successful relationships is communication, why don't we always do it well and consistently? We learned how to communicate based on our culture, family dynamics, and parents. Unfortunately, those models may not have always been the most productive or positive.

My family (Bryan) consisted of my two younger brothers and my mother. We did not have a lot of disagreements and things were typically pretty calm in our house. Disagreements were usually settled by wrestling it out as kids, sometimes playing the blame game as adults, or just simply moving on from the whole ordeal. Growing up, my family (Tam) consisted of my mother, stepfather, and three younger sisters, and our house was extremely loud. We talked loud, played loud, laughed loud, and most assuredly disagreed loudly. So you can only imagine marrying someone with a completely different communication style.

It took us many years to adapt to each other's way of communicating and to find our rhythm. There were times when one of us wanted to talk through a disagreement while the other didn't. The spouse who wanted to talk pushed and pushed until a blow-up ensued. As if released from a warplane, word bombs carpeted our home. The person who blew up would then say, "Well, you wanted me to talk." So, you can only guess how the other spouse felt, shocked and in awe by what just transpired and, as a result, they either withdrew or hid their feelings. We are not saying we don't still have "spirited conversations" and disagreements from time to time because we do; they are just fewer and farther between now. After 21 years, we've learned practical strategies to honor each other's need for space and to respect our unique differences of opinion and communication styles. We didn't start out that way but learned how to put into place practical ways of interacting during those "heated" moments.

Below are a few keys we've learned over the years and share with couples to help them along on their journey when having "spirited conversations" or disagreements.

Communication Key
1 – Timing is Everything

For the spouse who desires to address and resolve the issue during a disagreement, if your spouse communicates to you they no longer want to continue the conversation, please respect their wishes. Some spouses have used their desire to continue the conversation to force their spouse to engage. Depending on their personality, this may not be the best strategy. Attempting to force your spouse to talk when they no longer want to causes an elevated level of anxiety, frustration, anger, and possibly resentment. As a result, your spouse may shut down, withdraw, or decide it is better not to share with you how they feel at all to avoid future disagreements. Allow them time to discuss the matter, possibly later that night or the next day, especially if voices were raised, and you find it hard to see their point of view. This allows them the opportunity to gather their thoughts and cool down. Once you've given each other some time to process, ask them when they feel would be a better time to talk again. If you ask them in the heat of the moment, they are likely to respond, "Never," so timing is everything.

Communication Key
2 - Sooner Is Better Than Never

For the spouse who does not wish to talk because it may look like the beginning of a heated exchange (or you're in the thick of it), let your spouse know you need a time out. However, this is not a time to escape, ignore, or fail to address the issue. You should give your spouse a time that you are willing to come back and resolve the disagreement. If your spouse is seeking to talk about or resolve the issue, they need an opportunity to express how they feel and seek closure, similar to your need to take a time-out. As soon as you both feel you're ready, commit some time to actively resolving the matter in a mature and loving way so that you both feel heard. If you sweep the issue under the rug, nine times out of ten the issue will resurface again.

Communication Key
3 - Feel Free To Disagree

Give each other the freedom to share a difference of opinion. There is no rulebook that says you have to agree on everything and feel the same way. Differences of opinion do not have to affect the friendship or intimacy. However, if one spouse attempts to force the other to take their side on a matter, it will affect your friendship. Good relationships work at appreciating both your differences and similarities. The more freedom you give each other to express yourselves, the more you'll both feel valued. As you move in the same direction, the freedom you give will be reciprocated, causing a deeper level of intimacy.

Communication Key
4 - Read The Room

The ability to be honest with yourself and your spouse is the foundation of a healthy marriage. Relationship expert Dr. Gary Chapman writes in his book, *Now, You're Speaking My Language*, both spouses should be allowed to speak the truth in love. Throughout the different moments within the conversation, you should be reading the room and observing your spouse. If you observe your spouse is open to receiving what you're saying, allow yourself to be honest with them about how you are feeling or perceiving the situation. You don't need to nor should you say 'everything' that comes to your mind, however frustrated you may be. You want to be wise and leave room for a recovery conversation following the disagreement. It may be harder to recover the friendship if you are not mindful of words that could possibly damage your spouse's heart or feelings.

Keep in mind your spouse's temperament, personality, and where they are in this stage of the marriage. Are they currently feeling rejected? Insecure? Angry? Is something taking place in their life they are struggling with? Now is not the time to pull out word daggers and twist. Timing is key. Ask yourself, *will what I'm about to say take the conversation and relationship in a different direction?*

If you listen closely enough, with God's help, He will tell you when to stop talking or what not to say. Have you ever had heard "something" tell you, "Don't say that?" "You shouldn't do that?" That is God gently directing you. Follow His voice. He will help you communicate with your spouse. You just need to be willing to listen. He is on your side and wants your marriage and friendship to flourish. Even if you are not on a spiritual path, it is vital to make sure that you leave your relationship intact after every conversation with your spouse. We used this verse in the early years of our marriage to help keep our words in check.

"The one who has knowledge uses words with restraint, and whoever has understanding is even-tempered. Even fools are thought to be wise if they keep silent and discerning if they hold their tongue."

Proverbs 17:27 (NIV)

Just as it is impossible to unring a bell, unbridled words spoken without restraint can take a lifetime to heal.

Communication Key
5 - You Determine Your Access Level

As we mentioned earlier, all married couples are provided a key and we determine the level of access to our spouse's heart. If your spouse's heart is closed, there may be things you can do to gain access. During a particular season in the marriage, there may be a time when your spouse's heart is closed due to personal or past issues. In those instances, professional counseling can be sought or schedule a time to meet with a mature couple who can help you navigate the challenges you are facing. Even when we have access to our spouse's heart, will we always get it right? Will we always be 100% perfect in our responses and attitude? Absolutely not.

Not even a skilled professional gets it right one hundred percent of the time, so don't be so hard on yourself or your spouse. Open your heart and give your spouse grace to discover who you are. Sometimes the grace that you give will seem to be undeserved, but give it to them anyway. You may find that you will need the same grace you granted someday. If we do not want our spouse to erect a locked fortress around their heart, use words that unlock rather than lock.

Here are just a few examples of 'word keys' that can close access and open access to your spouse's heart and your relationship.

Word Keys That Lock and Close Access to Your Spouse Are:

1. **Disrespectful** – "You shouldn't eat that; you're getting fat."
2. **Critical** – "You never…"
3. **Judgmental** – "You always…"
4. **Unsupportive** – "That's a good idea, but…"
5. **Selfish** – "Well, I'm sorry, you're just going to have to deal with it."
6. **Sarcastic** – "Thanks … for nothing."

Can you imagine hearing the "click" from the locks of a spouse's heart as they hear those words spoken to them? Some spouses say these things oftentimes because of anger, frustration, unmet expectations, and, if we're honest, out of immaturity or selfishness. No one deserves to be demeaned, and the spouse on the receiving end should begin establishing boundaries to protect his or her heart by sharing what is and what is not acceptable.

We probably would not have said these words to our prospective spouse while engaged, so why would we do it after marriage? Lack of honor? Lack of respect? Lack of love? When these types of words are used, not only does it cause the spouse who said these words to be locked out, but the receiving spouse's feelings are now locked in. As a result, they are forced to internalize what was said, playing it over and over in their heads. Now feeling emotionally distant, they may resolve to avoid confrontation or not communicate at all. They may wonder, "Is that how they really feel?" "Do they love me?" "Did I make the right decision marrying this person?" The list goes on and on.

We've all probably experienced wanting to share our feelings in a relationship but decided not to because we were afraid of the reaction or response we might receive. Our inability to share on a deeper level can cause loneliness and isolation for one or both spouses. Failing to share your thoughts and feelings with the one you love indicates a loss of trust or support, and it will take additional effort to rectify and turn the relationship around.

After years of research, Dr. John Gottman, relationship psychologist and marriage guru, found that the difference between a happy and an unhappy marriage is a 5:1 ratio. He essentially writes all couples should have five times more positive interactions than negative for a happy relationship to thrive. In other words, as long as the couple is experiencing five times more positive encounters than negative, the relationship is likelier to be happier and more stable. On the other hand, he discovered couples who had more negative encounters than positive were usually unhappy, emotionally distant, and teetering on the brink of divorce. Negative interactions occur in a happy and healthy relationship, as well. Still, it seems couples that are happier work together to repair, recover from, and replace their negative experiences with more productive and happier ones. So as you can see, words are powerful and determine the direction your marriage will go.

We've taken a look at few keys that do not allow access; now let's take a look at words and language that give a spouse access.

Word Keys That Unlock and Provide Access to Your Spouse Are:

1. **Respectful** – "I trust your judgment."
2. **Affirming** – "You did a great job."
3. **Appreciative** – "Do you know what I appreciate about you____?"
4. **Encouraging** – "You got this. We're in this together."
5. **Supportive** – "Let me know how I can help you."
6. **Empathetic** – "Tell me more about…"

Can you imagine the open access a spouse can receive as they say or hear these words spoken to them? They can be music to your spouse's ears because these words protect, respect, and affirm love. Words such as these are powerful and have the ability to build emotional intimacy and bonds that cannot be easily broken. Just as negative words can block access, these words can breathe life back into the heart of your spouse and marriage. You can say these words to them and they will never grow tired of hearing them. Everyone wants to be loved, so use these words to strengthen your relationship. They will give you the ability to break through barriers that attempt to hinder you from reaching your destination.

FUELING YOU TRUST TANK

During the first few years of our marriage, we handled money pretty poorly. A "me" and "mine" mindset from our many years being single and independent carried over into our marriage. We'd spend and spend, failing to create a family budget, and when we did, we failed to follow it consistently. We were surprised to see late notices and insufficient funds fee charges. We also didn't entirely trust each other when it came to money. We either didn't trust each other to actually pay the bills or trust the other to be transparent about where the money was spent or located. It was a mess. We then began doing little things to "protect" ourselves from each other, slowly siphoning the trust we initially had for one another when we entered the marriage. After a while, the little things became big things, and not only was our bank account on "E", but so was our marriage.

Is Your Trust Tank Full?

So, what is trust? Trust is a feeling of safety and the ability to place confidence in the one you love. The trust you have chosen to give your spouse attests, they have proven to be consistent in their character and dependability. Just as the right communication keys ensure you have access, trust gives the marriage the fuel it needs to stay on course. It requires the couples to ask themselves very specific questions that can only be answered through *actions*.

33

Trust Asks:

- Do you accept me?
- Can I depend on you?
- Will you be faithful to me?
- Will you be there if I need you?
- Will you always be honest with me?
- Am I safe to move forward with you?
- Will you have my back in front of others?
- Will you stay consistent in your love for me?
- Will you do the right thing when I'm not around?

Trust is like striking oil in your marriage and should be guarded at all costs. It's a valuable commodity that gives couples the fuel they need to go the distance. Here are just a few ways to add trust fuel to your marriage:

1. Keep Your Word

This seems quite obvious, but it may be one of the hardest, especially if you have been married for a long period of time or if you have a spouse that is more easygoing. It is easy for a spouse to say to themselves "well if I don't do it, they will understand." We don't want to take advantage of the grace granted by failing to keep our word. Also, you may be tempted to want to appease your spouse by telling them you can follow through on a commitment you know you may not be able to. Tell them the truth; when you fail to do so, they may experience unnecessary disappointment if you cannot fulfill what was promised.

2. Don't Withhold Details

The quickest way to lose the trust that you gained is to tell a lie or withhold details that should be shared with your spouse. When you are not honest, your spouse is forced to play Inspector Gadget and wade through all of the minutiae trying to get to the bottom of things. What could have taken five minutes merely sharing a few details, now takes hours and even days to iron out. Even if it hurts, tell the truth and share pertinent details because it will eventually come out.

We sparred and played the bob and weave game for many years, especially when it came to money. We finally had to decide to be upfront and honest about our lack of trust for one another. We fessed up to where the money was being spent so that we could dig ourselves out of a hole and correct the problem. Once we were honest with each other, things began to turn around in our marriage, we also began to trust each other more, and our finances improved significantly over time.

3. Admit Mistakes

Admitting that we are wrong can be a bit intimidating and scary at times. We tend to clam up when we realize we have to admit our mistakes to our spouse. We can be tempted to debate being forthcoming about our mistakes because we believe, "I may hear this again," or that it may be held against you. Everyone wants to be right, but spouses who can freely admit their mistakes even the playing field. It says neither of us is perfect and allows room for everyone to open the door to grace. A grace-rich marriage works not to point fingers but can admit they missed it. This ability to extend grace allow spouses to be vulnerable without fear of judgment or criticism.

4. Vulnerability Is Valuable

Expressing your feelings and being transparent is an invaluable gift you can give to your spouse. It says, "I am laying my heart out and I trust you with it." When spouses show their vulnerability, they are essentially peeling off invisible layers, allowing themselves to be discovered and understood. It can be seen as a great risk for the spouse who decides to share their heart, so it is vital we are good stewards of their feelings. If your spouse senses rejection as a result of what they've shared, they may be reluctant to share their feelings in the future. However, if what they've shared is received with acceptance and empathy, you are filling their trust tank and creating opportunities for a greater level of intimacy in your relationship.

YOUR STORY

Communication Keys and Trust Tank Exercise

1. After reading this chapter, how would you rate the communication between you and your spouse? Based on a scale of 1-5 (1-We could use a bit of help to 5 - We're both open books.)

Your score: _____

What is your spouse's score? _____

2. What are two ways you can improve your communication if your rating is between 1–4?

_____

_____

3. Being vulnerable can be a bit scary at times however, it is important to understand your spouse's needs and for them to understand yours. Share with your spouse two things you need from them. Make sure it is something they are capable of doing. Ask them how often they

need what was requested and times they feel they may need it the most. (i.e., alone time, attention, intimacy)

My Spouse Needs:

1. _____

2. _____

I Need:

1. _____

2. _____

4. In what ways can you begin meeting those needs? What can you do first? (Hint: Ask your spouse)

_____

_____

5. List four ways you can fill up each other's trust tank. (i.e. Acknowledge feelings)

_____

_____

_____

_____

HOMEWORK CHALLENGE #2

Tell Me Something Good

Catch your spouse doing something good this week. For the next seven days, when your spouse follows through on a promise or does something you didn't ask or expect, find a quiet moment and thank them. Tell them how much you appreciated what they did.

Did you complete the questions and homework challenge?

If you did, then you and your spouse should reward yourselves. Choose a small gift and surprise your spouse with it or switch out a chore your spouse is not particularly fond of. Choose to do something they really love.

We commit to rewarding ourselves this week by:

_____

You have your keys and your tanks are full! Now let's begin our journey, but remember to watch out for potholes on the road to romance!

Chapter Three

Discovering Your Spouse on the Journey

*H*ave you ever driven long distances with family members or friends? If you have for example, driven from the East Coast to the South or up the California coast, at the outset of the trip, you may notice everyone is always extremely thrilled because of the exciting new adventure up ahead. After a while, exhaustion sets in, and the travelers seem to forget about the once anticipated destination. The excursion seems to lose its luster, and small things about the car's occupants soon begin to irritate us. The spouse chosen to be the navigator has quickly turned into the "naggi-vator" and the songs that used to keep everyone's spirits up now annoy their once captive audience. What happened? The occupants lost the joy of expectancy or possibly failed to anticipate the challenges they'd be required to adapt to along the way.

Beginning a new journey is always fun and exciting. However, after experiencing a lengthy lull in the trip or a few challenges along the way, this may tempt one to rethink or question whether they made the right decision taking the trip. These feelings can also occur in marriage and usually takes place after the proverbial honeymoon stage is over. When we enter a new season or territory in our marriage, the landscape tends to change, and we are forced to adapt to those changes sometimes rather quickly. During these times, we tend to forget what attracted us to our spouse, things we loved about our friendship, and the many reasons why we decided to venture out on this marital journey together.

Conflicts and misunderstandings may occur throughout the journey from time to time but should not be mistaken nor mislabeled as a problem in your marriage. They are merely season changes. These are also times and opportunities to grow and adapt to each other's personal bents. As you work on resolving the issues and adapting, keep in mind the rewards that await you are far better than what you may be experiencing during challenging times.

When Opposites ~~Attack~~ Attract

What attracted you to your spouse? Was it their smile? Good looks? Charismatic personality? Calm demeanor? All marriages have their own stamp of uniqueness and we usually find what attracted us to our spouse are personality traits that may be much different than ours. Have you ever noticed in a relationship one person is an introvert while the other is an extrovert? One likes to socialize; and the other is a homebody? Or one is a spender, and the other wants to save for the future, and the list goes on. Isn't it strange that we tend to date and marry people who are our polar opposites? These core qualities and differences are what attracted us to our spouse.

When we're dating, our differences are not as apparent during the initial stages of the relationship. If you have a Type-A personality prone to focusing on time management and the urgency of matters, you may have admired the steadiness your soon-to-be spouse brought to the relationship. You valued their calm demeanor and steady pace because you know your Type-A personality can be a little over the top at times. However, that admiration may have quickly turned into exasperation when you discovered your new spouse's "personality strengths" decided to shine through and kick into high gear at the most inopportune time. You then found yourself slightly irritated as they meandered throughout the house slow as Mississippi molasses, looking for their shoes or wallet. It drove you a little crazy, right?

Do you admire your spouse's love for adventure? While you were dating, it was so exciting to see them so early in the morning, and you'd get up at first light to have morning breakfast with them at their favorite neighborhood diner. Then you realize after the honeymoon that you, the non-morning person and quintessential night hawk, are now married to Susie or Sammy Sunshine. To your amazement, you discover they still want you to go on a hike with them at 5:00 a.m., then on to the farmer's market, and immediately after that, they make a bee line over to their favorite breakfast spot because the day has just begun.

We've all experienced some version of these scenarios and may have fallen into the trap of thinking this will all change and one day, they'll slow down (or speed up) eventually once we get married. However, they feel quite the opposite; in their minds, they are relishing the thought, *I get to do what I love, with the person I love on a more frequent basis!* They did not change; our expectations did. So how do we navigate our differences without going a little stir crazy in the process? When we encountered many of the same examples, such as missing each other's queues or not understanding one another's expectations, we knew we needed to learn how to adapt and not attack the very personality traits we had come to admire and love. First, we received guidance from the Bible based on our core beliefs in the Word of God. We found that scriptures act as a mirror and exposes your heart in every situation. We began following what the scriptures were encouraging us to do in the areas of patience, forgiveness, and kindness, which is a lifelong commitment we continue to practice daily.

Don't just listen to God's word. You must do what it says. Otherwise, you are only fooling yourselves. For if you listen to the word and don't obey, it is like glancing at your face in a mirror. You see yourself, walk away, and forget what you look like. But if you look carefully into the perfect law that sets you free, and if you do what it says and don't forget what you heard, then God will bless you for doing it.

James 1:22–25 (NLT)

Rediscovering Your Spouse

Those were the spiritual steps we walked through. We also knew we needed to find strategies that helped us to understand and adapt to each other's personality styles while on this lifelong journey. We decided to use the DISC personality profile assessment in our discovery process. This practical tool gave us an opportunity to take a closer look at our own behavior, strengths, and even weaknesses. This was an important process because it helped us recalibrate the direction we were headed in, as well as accept, appreciate, and adapt to each other's unique personality differences.

The DISC assessment is broken into four common personality behaviors and is used to determine how individuals typically interact with others, their style of communication, how they presumably react in certain situations, and how they handle conflict. The DISC profile was created by psychologist Dr. William Marston whose research theorized that the way we express ourselves and relate to others can be categorized into four distinct behaviors:

D - Dominant
I - Influencing
S - Steady
C - Conscientious

The goal is for you to discover not only your personality profile but your spouse's as well; and find positive ways to adapt to their style and vice versely. Communication is the greatest asset in any relationship, so your ability to adapt to each other's style will help you both learn what's important to each other and discover approaches that may be effective or ineffective when communicating.

Let's take a look at the four distinct profiles and see if you can identify your personality profile first and then your spouse's.

D - Personality Profile (Direct)
Decisive, Problem Solver, Self-Starter

Common Characteristics

⊙ Prefers independence

⊙ Likes to get to the point

⊙ Makes decisions quickly

⊙ Deals with conflict head-on

⊙ Likes to take control and lead

⊙ Dislikes routine and can be bored easily

⊙ Can sometimes be more task-oriented than people-oriented

D – Strengths & Challenges	
D – Strengths	**D – Challenges**
· Focuses on results · Communicates directly · Resilient in the face of fear · Has the ability to motivate others · Committed to getting things done	· Can be impatient · Prone to being argumentative · Takes on too much at once · May fail to include others · Can be critical at times

A Few Things to Remember
When Communicating with Your D - Spouse

⊙ Provide options and alternatives to help make decisions

⊙ They like it when you get to the point when communicating

⊙ When explaining, try to avoid tangents, bunny trails and things that are off-topic

⊙ If you disagree, focus on "what" instead of the "how" they dislike too many details

⊙ They are problem solvers, so be prepared to offer a solution. If you focus on the negative and say why something can't be done, they may see you as a complainer and negative

How You Can Help Your D - Spouse

⊙ Let them know you appreciate them listening (when they do)

⊙ Attempt to use a light-hearted tone to deescalate the conflict

⊙ Use a give and take method by being gentle yet firm on your decision

⊙ Negotiate with them: "You choose X this time; I'll choose Y next time"

⊙ Calmly and confidently tell them how their behavior is making you feel

⊙ Remind your spouse how their behavior is affecting you or the situation

⊙ If you don't feel comfortable with the situation or decision made, explain and repeat if necessary.

⊙ D's are strong-willed so don't be afraid to articulate, "I'm not comfortable with that decision," "I don't see it that way," "That's not something I'm comfortable with," "I'm comfortable with X, Y, or Z," "Which one would you prefer?"

D - Growth Opportunities

⊙ Ask for others' opinions and insights
⊙ Spend quality time with those who need it
⊙ Slow down and work on avoiding rushing others
⊙ Practice letting go of control and encourage creativity
⊙ Ask yourself: *If I were on the other end of this decision or conversation, how would I feel?*
⊙ Share your intent and talk to others before you change plans that may affect them

What Motivates Your D-Spouse?

D's are motivated by setting and achieving goals they set for themselves and others. They appreciate being recognized for their hard work and value they bring to the relationship. They need a great deal of freedom from the mundane and repetitious, so try not to box them in. They are highly motivated when they can make decisions and are free to take risks. D's also have an innate need to quickly change ineffective processes or things within their environment when it becomes too stagnant, dull, or routine.

I-Personality Profile – (Influencer)
Fun, Optimistic, Talkative

Common Characteristics

⊙ Charming

⊙ Persuasive

⊙ Enthusiastic

⊙ Spontaneous

⊙ Great encourager

⊙ Great sense of humor

⊙ Likes to be admired and loves attention

I – Strengths & Challenges	
I – Strengths	**I – Challenges**
· Highly intuitive · Very optimistic · Can quickly improvise if difficulties arise · Brings high energy and fun to all relationships · Emotionally expressive and a great communicator	· Can be very disorganized · Can be impatient when working through problems · May not have a great deal of follow through · Likes to persuade others toward their way of thinking · More concerned with fun and socializing than the details

A Few Things to Remember
When Communicating with Your I - Spouse

⊙ Plan time to socialize

⊙ Don't leave decisions up in the air

⊙ Listen to them and don't do all the talking

⊙ Use humor and a casual tone when speaking

⊙ Don't react to them in a way that makes them feel rejected

⊙ They are great problem solvers, so don't leave them out of the decision-making process

How You Can Help Your I - Spouse

⊙ Pitch in to help them with one task at a time

⊙ Offer to assist them with getting more organized, but don't demand

⊙ Remind them of issues that may arise if you see they are slow to action

⊙ Do your part in assisting them to stay focused and discuss the details with them

⊙ Help them see how their lack of planning or focus may be affecting you or others

I - Growth Opportunities

⊙ Focus more on the details and the facts

⊙ Be open to listening to other's opinions

⊙ Practice patience and empathize with others

⊙ Plan out your ideas by making lists and prioritizing

⊙ Use time wisely, failure to do so may negatively impact others

What Motivates Your I-Spouse?

I's love attention, so they are motivated by praise, acceptance, and quality time. They are driven by freedom and fun, so make sure they have plenty of time to socialize. I's love independence, so don't have too many rules. They are born collaborators and have the natural ability to motivate others. They love people, a fast pace, and results.

S – Personality Profile (Steady)
Stable, Loyal, Predictable

Common Characteristics

⊙ Playful

⊙ Reserved

⊙ Difficult to "read"

⊙ Can be introverted

⊙ Not very emotional

⊙ Tendency to be quiet

⊙ Values fairness and justice

S – Strengths & Challenges	
S – Strengths	**S – Challenges**
· Empathetic · Good listeners · Defenders of those they love · Responds to the needs of others · Desire to reconcile when conflicts arise	· Resistant to change · Sensitive to criticism · Finds it difficult to say no · Has a tendency to hold grudges · Can be easily taken advantage of

A Few Things to Remember
When Communicating with Your S - Spouse

⊙ Be attentive to their needs

⊙ Ask specific questions about how they are feeling

⊙ Show sincere interest in their goals, dreams, and desires

⊙ Build trust by not promising something you can't deliver on

⊙ Listen when they are speaking, they dislike being interrupted

⊙ Do not speak harshly to this personality, they can be sensitive

⊙ They dislike change, so share with them ahead of time if you are thinking of changing the initial plan. Most importantly, share with them the reason why the plans are changing

How You Can Help Your S - Spouse

⊙ Let them know it's ok to say no

⊙ Encourage them to focus on their needs

⊙ Help them to tap into their sense of humor by pointing out funny observations

⊙ Spend quality time with them on their terms; this may be at home or in a quiet setting

⊙ Reassure your spouse you are not criticizing them; but that you are seeking a solution you can both live with

⊙ Encourage them to verbalize their feelings and demonstrate you care based on your actions, not your words

⊙ They need alone time, allow them to process. However, ask them for a time when you both can talk about the issue in an effort to resolve it

S - Growth Opportunities

⊙ Don't be afraid to face issues head-on. Assert yourself in the decision making process

⊙ Remember you may be married to a different personality type that may not enjoy routine, so try new things your spouse may be interested in

⊙ Remember, people are not perfect and may disappoint you. Focus on forgiveness if you desire growth in the relationship

⊙ Don't forget you are valuable and loved. You do not have to tolerate behaviors that attempt to take advantage of you; it's okay to say no and speak up for yourself

What Motivates Your S - Spouse?

S's are motivated by positive and productive relationships. They love when everyone is getting along and in harmony. Their motivation is safety and security, so it is important to be truthful with them at all times. If you need to change plans, be sure to give them a heads-up with enough time to process. It is sometimes challenging for them to get out of their routine, so be patient with them. Remember that they put people before themselves and may become quietly resentful if they feel you did not consider their feelings.

C – Personality Profile (Conscientious)
Creative, Systematic, Precise

Common Characteristics

⊙ Perfectionist

⊙ Detail-Oriented

⊙ Introverted

⊙ Analytical

⊙ Compliant

⊙ Even-tempered

⊙ Focused

C – Strengths & Challenges	
C – Strengths	**C – Challenges**
· Tends to be diplomatic · Relates well with others · Is comfortable with conflict when finding a solution · Takes time to think things through before they react · Observes and collects data to help make decisions	· Desires to always be right · Can be critical and faultfinding · Prefers not to verbalize feelings · May overcomplicate problems with solutions · Can be pessimistic and temperamental

A Few Things to Remember
When Communicating with Your C - Spouse

⊙ Give them space

⊙ Give them lots of details

⊙ Express confidence in them

⊙ Do not force a quick decision

⊙ Say thank you and appreciate their efforts

⊙ Be patient they need lots of time to process

⊙ Avoid criticism that attacks them personally

⊙ Avoid explaining things with too much emotion

⊙ Ask them how they are feeling about the issue and allow them an opportunity to process

How You Can Help Your C - Spouse

⊙ Reassure them it's okay to be open and vulnerable at times

⊙ Remind them that human error can be reduced not eliminated

⊙ Gently encourage them to be less critical and more light-hearted

⊙ Be sure that you can be trusted with their feelings as they can be sensitive

⊙ Encourage them to share their feelings and be willing to listen in a calm manner when they are explaining themselves

C - Growth Opportunities

⊙ Resist isolating yourself, people need your keen mind and tender heart

⊙ Don't be afraid to make mistakes, they are learning and growth opportunities

⊙ Remember to remain open minded and flexible because everyone has natural differences in talents and abilities

⊙ You may need to free yourself up and not put so much on your plate. Let go of analysis paralysis and delegate a few more tasks

What Motivates Your C - Spouse?

C's are motivated by logic and have high standards. They are sticklers for the rules and usually see most things in black and white. Gray areas may not be tolerated. They love to showcase their expertise, knowledge, and quality of work so be sure to recognize when your spouse is doing something well. They thrive in non-confrontational relationships, so do your best to pursue peace with this personality style.

YOUR STORY

Commit to learning more about your spouse's personality and communication style. It may feel a bit awkward at first but work towards adapting to their personality style. Adaptability and flexibility does not mean you are being disingenuous with how you feel; it's an attempt to bring out the best in your spouse and give your marriage a chance to grow.

We all have a blend of the profiles and a dominant personality trait.

1. What is your dominant personality profile?

_____

2. What is your spouse's personality profile?

_____

3. How are your personalities similar?

_____

4. In what areas are you notably different?

_____

5. How can your differences be a strength in your marriage?

_____

6. From the "A few things to remember" section, ask your spouse how they would like you to communicate with them. Write their responses below.

_____

_____

_____

_____

HOMEWORK CHALLENGE #3

I See You

This week, commit to asking each other how well you are communicating and responding based on the personality profile lists provided. If there are times when you did not respond well, seek ways to improve daily. Focus on your successes and ask each other what you liked about your interaction this week.

Also, thank your spouse if they had a tough week, were patient, and worked hard toward being flexible and adaptive.

Did you do the homework Challenge?

If you did, reward yourselves. Do something spontaneous this week!

We commit to rewarding ourselves by:

You're doing great! You've avoided those communication potholes. Now, be sure to keep your eyes open, you don't want to miss your exit!

Chapter Four

Distractions, Delays, & The Mojave Desert

*I*n the summer of 2019, we found ourselves stuck in California's Mojave Desert on my birthday of all days. What should have been a scenic 4.5-hour adventurous drive turned into eight hot hellacious hours. After attending a fantastic service that morning at L.A. One Church, we left L.A. and planned a drive to Las Vegas to stay in one of the lavish hotels along the Las Vegas Strip. I wanted Bryan to see the Fountains of Bellagio he'd always admired in the movie *Ocean's 11* as I had done on many occasions while traveling for work.

After stopping for a treasure trove of snacks, we plotted our course and headed towards our destination. Admiring the picturesque mountains of California, I noticed Bryan seemed distracted. We were moving extremely fast, Formula-1 Lewis Hamilton fast, and time seemed to stand still as we passed our exit and began heading in a new direction. The words "There's the exit" were trapped in my throat but didn't stay there for long. At that moment, I saw our dreams of getting to Las Vegas on time go up in smoke.

"You just missed the exit!" "What happened?" "You have a G.P.S!" "You weren't paying attention!" "You know today is my birthday, right?" barraged my poor husband. The man of steady nerves and the patience of Job dissipated before my very eyes. I had gotten on his last nerve. I wanted to show him a good time, and he ruined it, the nerve! (Anger makes you think rationally, right?) Then the man with the patience of Job went on to share with me a few choice words. I then shared a few more choice words with him, and our cache of communication strategies simply flew out the window, right into the desert.

There we were, in the middle of one of the hottest deserts known to man, on one of the hottest days of the year in late August. As quickly as the argument began, it suddenly stopped. The only sound I could hear was my voice trailing off and the radio losing its reception as we moved progressively toward the most massive mounds of earth I had ever seen. At that moment, I became keenly aware of everything around me. There was a sea of cars in front of and behind us and a handful stuck on the side of the road. As the cars slowed down, we began to realize we were no longer moving; we were in a traffic jam in the middle of the desert! I thought to myself, *this is not what we planned. We just left church for goodness' sake, it's my birthday, and I hope our car does not overheat.* My mind began to race at the thought of breaking down on the side of the road. It would have been next to impossible to receive assistance because we were surrounded on all sides and the traffic jam stretched for miles over the mountains. I resolved we were going to have to put this birthday in the history books.

After the radio finally lost all reception, we traveled at a snail's pace at nearly three mph (no kidding, I looked) in total silence. Can you imagine how awkward it is to sit in a car in total silence for hours in the middle of the desert? I probably would have held out not talking to him for the duration of the trip if it were not for that darn radio! Nevertheless, I finally came to myself and realized how selfish I had been. Presumably, I didn't account for delays or human error in my plan. It's funny how we are not nearly as hard on ourselves when we make mistakes as we are on others when they do.

"Do you think those people on the side of the road would like some water?" and "Let's listen to the message we heard earlier today," was how the conversation began. Stepping out to clear the air allowed us to initiate the process of apologizing. We apologized for the way we had spoken to each other, and I apologized for my selfishness and lack of grace. So after a great deal of apologizing and the reassurance of love, we took the opportunity to enjoy a beautiful sunset descending over the dusty mounds of the Mojave.

WATCH OUT FOR DELAYS

Being distracted by unimportant things that do not move your marriage forward can cause significant delays. In our case, we probably should have paid closer attention and worked together, but we failed to do that. This would have prevented an ugly disagreement and made for a more pleasant experience earlier in our journey. As a result of this delay, we did not have an opportunity to see the sites we'd planned because the detour extended our time in the desert. We'd never driven that stretch of highway before, so we needed each other more than ever during that time. Failing to consider one another and work together causes delays, resulting in holding patterns that keep you and your spouse from moving forward to the destination you both desire.

As you venture out on this journey, there will be roads you'll travel together that you and your spouse may not be familiar with. During those times, it is especially important to remain close and vigilant to prevent delays. These delays can impact the friendship within your marriage for years if you are not aware of the many issues that may cause them. We discovered two delays that kept us and the numerous couples we've coached from enjoying the marriage they desired for many years. Those two delays are selfishness and unforgiveness.

This section may be a bit bumpy for some, but it will be beneficial. The purpose is not to point fingers because we are all fallible human beings in need of grace. The goal is to highlight areas where a bit of strengthening may be required and establish ways you and your spouse can continue to grow in friendship and love.

The #1 Cause of Delay: Selfishness

After many years of together, couples may begin to develop bouts of amnesia from time to time. We forget to be generous with our words, patience, time, possessions, and respect. Over time, if we're not careful, we can forget the value we once held for our spouse, the sacrifices of love that seemed effortless while dating, and begin to place our needs above our spouse's. As we proudly notch anniversary years under our belts, our spouses can become all too familiar to us. We can begin treating them like a common household fixture that we walk past daily. Unconsciously, we may become careless with our words, dismissive of their physical and emotional needs, and assume they are "fine," telling ourselves, *they will love me regardless of my actions.* That is what selfishness does. It causes us to take our spouses for granted, forgetting the vows we made to honor, love, and cherish.

We've all experienced moments of selfishness, demanding our way, or subtly expecting our spouse to give us what we want, how we want it, when we want it, preferably with a smile and on a silver platter. We usually don't go into marriage thinking we're going to become selfish. There may be a minuscule amount of selfishness still lying dormant within us before getting married, but it is suppressed by the love cocktail of hormones we discussed in the earlier chapter.

You can spot selfishness very early in the life of a child if you pay close enough attention. During our primary school years, we're taught to share, be considerate of others, and help those around us. Many of us may remember our teachers admonishing, "Suzie, everyone gets a turn," "Please share your purple crayon with Billy," or, "Please thank Mrs. Kelly for bringing in snacks today." However, when we are admonished by our spouse to be considerate, share, and say thank you twenty, thirty, or even forty years later, it becomes a more significant issue in our relationship that must be addressed and worked through.

Selfishness takes a marriage off course, tempting a spouse to head for the nearest exit when requests, pleas, and threats have fallen on deaf ears for years. In extreme cases, it says in both *words* and *actions*:

- "I am important and you are not"
- "My way is better than your way"
- "I don't care what you want or need"
- "My needs will always come before yours"
- "My needs must be considered at all times"
- "I only care about my feelings and yours do not matter"
- "I'm the only person who matters in this relationship"
- "What I have to do is more important; what you have to do can take a back seat"
- "I may get to what's important to you eventually, and if I don't, you'll get over it"

These words may sound harsh, but they are unfortunately said to spouses every day verbally or by way of a spouse's actions. The damage associated with these words leaves a spouse feeling alone, helpless, and unimportant. You can say with your words that you love your spouse, but your actions and how you make them feel is what will always be believed. Author and poet Maya Angelou eloquently attested to this fact in her quote, *"I've learned that people will forget what you said, people will forget what you did, but people will never forget how you made them feel."* Our actions, words, and how we make our spouses feel will always determine the course of our marriage.

Signs of Selfishness

We read a few extreme cases above. Below are just a few common scenarios many couples face when dealing with selfishness in marriage.

1. The Need to Always Be Right

When you focus on being right, someone inevitably has to be wrong. Attempting to prove you are right turns the conversation into a courtroom drama where you attempt to convince your spouse that without a reasonable doubt, their thinking is flawed. We don't want to present our spouse with a litany of evidence dating back five years to prove we are right. In the end when we do this, we sentence our spouse to a lifelong prison term of feeling devalued and unimportant.

2. Commandeering the Conversation

One spouse may be more prone to hijack the conversation by continually interrupting their spouse because they do not want to hear their perspective. When we cut our spouses off and don't allow them to speak, we are essentially saying, "You don't deserve to be heard." A conversation is a dialogue and both spouses' perspective deserves to be considered.

3. Combat Mode

How do you react if your spouse shares with you how your actions are negatively impacting them? Do you get defensive? Angry? Blame? Deny? Lash out? If your spouse has not recently shared with you how your behavior impacts them and your marriage, could it be they can't? Silence does not always mean acceptance or contentment. You didn't get married to enlist in a battle or constantly be at odds. You're on the same side; be willing to call a truce and stop the friendly fire.

4. Comfort Is King

Before you were married, did you attempt to move heaven and earth for your spouse but now find it difficult to move across the room to bring them the remote? Selfishness always finds it easy to say no or justifies why it cannot accommodate a need. If you are finding excuses for why you cannot work in partnership with your spouse because it requires more effort than you are willing to exert, you may still be living in a world of "me" and not "we."

The Genesis of Selfishness

We may exhibit selfish traits because we grew up in an environment where emotional, material, and financial needs were not met. The family dynamic may have been one of self-sufficiency with an "every man for himself" mentality requiring the spouse to fend for themselves. This scarcity mindset makes those prone to selfishness unwilling to give more than they receive because of fear of lack.

A more obvious reason is that it seems easier to give in to those who are more prone to selfishness. Desiring to avoid another fight, tantrum, or deal with the backlash, a spouse may eventually give in, which unfortunately further perpetuates the cycle. This cycle without intervention may be extremely difficult to stop or break. Selfishness is like a child who is seldom told no and once the parent finally doesn't give in to their demands or desires, drama ensues.

Unfortunately, it takes us being jolted out of our comfort zone to realize there is a problem. Oftentimes emotional and physical distance; and the loss of the relationship are all consequences of self-centeredness. This however, does not have to continue or cause a detour in your marriage. By choosing to make simple, intentional decisions every day, couples can recalibrate and set a new course for their marriage.

The Only Weapon That Defeats Selfishness

The greatest weapon against selfishness is sacrifice. You actually can see the benefits of it play out in our everyday lives. An athlete will sacrifice time in the gym to excel in a sport they love; a student sacrifices time with friends to pursue their dream career, or a parent will take on a second job to pay for extracurricular lessons because they recognize talent in their child. We can have that same passion for our spouse and make sacrifices seem effortless when we commit to doing it together and by putting each other first. It can seem like a tough task when it's one-sided, but it does not have to be.

For over twenty years, people have commented to us, "You both look so happy, what's the secret?" They are usually pretty shocked when we give them the answer, we work at out-giving one another. Out-giving and out-loving each other was something we learned to do during an extremely tough season in our marriage, which we share in the last chapter. We work at sacrificing our need to be right for the greater good of our relationship because we spent years trying to control each other, especially in the area of our finances, because we didn't always trust each other. "This is my money; you have yours, and I have mine," was a weekly conversation. Our relationship always seemed a little disjointed until we decided to trust and sacrifice our need for control.

Many years later, what was a game of out-giving has become a lifestyle and we could not do this without our faith in God. Again, you may not be on a spiritual journey. Still, we wholeheartedly believe the secret to making our marriage work and many others is based on certain principles. These principles are based on the love of Jesus and His example of how both men and women should love one another. He made the ultimate sacrifice with His life to show what true love is, and we can attest to these principles after 21 years. We decided to out-give, out-serve, and sacrifice for one another, based on the following scriptures:

"Husbands, love your wives, just as Christ loved the church and gave himself up for her. This same way, husbands ought to love their wives as their own bodies. He who loves his wife loves himself. After all, no one ever hated their own body, but they feed and care for their body, just as Christ does the church."

Ephesians 5:25, 28–29 (NIV)

"Do nothing out of selfish ambition or vain conceit. Rather, in humility value others above yourselves, not looking to your own interests but each of you to the interests of the others."

Philippians 2:3–4 (NIV)

"Greater love has no one than this: to lay down one's life for one's friends."

John 15:13 (NIV)

The greatest proof of love is sacrifice. Can you sacrifice your time? Money? Need to be right? There is beauty in sacrifice, that can be seen after you've been on the journey for a while. There will be certain mile markers on the journey where you will be able to look back and see the benefits, purpose, and how far you've come together. A valuable lesson in self-sacrifice changed the very trajectory and course of our friendship, relationship, and life.

Proof of Love

As a single woman, I prayed long and hard to be married and continued to pray even while I dated Bryan. I asked God to confirm in my heart if he was the man I should actually marry. I had seen so many marriages fail and as a young woman; and I'd imagined myself being more like Elizabeth Taylor marrying two, four, even six times until I'd finally gotten it right; but deep down, that's not what I wanted.

When Bryan and I first began dating, he would leave a dozen long-stemmed red roses in my car, surprising me many times in the early morning before going to work. Also, periodically, after leaving my apartment in the evening, he'd place cards in inconspicuous places for me to find. This all seemed so foreign to me. I'd simply dated before but was never courted, and it all seemed too good to be true. One day, sitting in my living room, I heard a small whisper in my heart and God saying to me, "I am loving you through him." My heart melted. *Wow, this is what courtship looks like and how much God loves me?* After dating several months, I still wasn't convinced he was my husband because I was still afraid all of the love and attention I was receiving would not last long. I was terrified of making a mistake and my greatest fear was marrying the wrong person relegated to living in a broken, unfulfilled marriage, feeling like a prisoner of war.

Within the same year, Bryan proposed and I accepted. However, deep down, I still was not convinced. I thought to myself, *Okay, this is great, he's great, but I don't want to make another mistake and end up with the wrong person. I cannot endure another heartbreak,* and I began to get very candid with God. I prayed, "Father listen, you have to let me know if this guy is the one, please do not tell me on the day of the wedding. I am not Julia Roberts, and I don't have time to reenact the scene from the movie *Runaway Bride,* please reassure my heart. I will let him go if he is not the one." I was serious about my resolve to let him go and prepared my heart for however God chose to answer.

A Surprising Sacrifice of Love

It had been a typical day when he arrived at my house. I knew we'd be going on one of our romantic adventures, but I immediately sensed something was wrong when I opened the door. I noticed something odd; his car was not parked in front of my house, which piqued my interest. He was still outside attempting to walk in, but something in me would not allow him to come in. I said, "Bryan, where is your car?"

With his eyes downcast, he said, "I don't have it now."

My mind raced a thousand miles per minute. *Does another woman have it? Did he fall in with some bad guys?* (I have no idea why I thought that) *Who is this man? It's a woman. I'm sure of it!* So many thoughts flooded my mind.

He must have seen the confusion on my face and steam coming out of my ears and quickly said, "My car was repossessed."

I was shocked, speechless, and my mind ran a thousand miles per minute. *How? Is he irresponsible? I'm not dealing with this! He's irresponsible! He can forget this wedding business!*

My mind continued to run wild and his words cut through my thoughts like a hot knife cutting through cold butter with one simple statement. "I want you to be my wife, and I stopped making my car payments, so they took my car. I used my car payment money to buy your engagement ring. I want you to be my wife."

The heavens opened and the angels sang! That was my answer, sacrifice. At that moment, I just knew. All of the prayers I prayed had culminated into this one moment. Everything that I had prayed for I was receiving and then some, but this was the confirmation I needed that settled my doubts. I thought to myself, *I don't think I've ever heard of any man sacrificing his car for love.* (He eventually did get his car back a few weeks later.)

In my heart, the Lord reminded me that true love is sacrifice. What He did for me on the cross is how a husband is supposed to love their wife. This level of sacrifice has been repeated over and over again throughout our marriage. Love and sacrifice are not just acts of kindness to rack up brownie points or a strategy to get back something in return. Sacrifice requires a risk of self. At that moment, my husband-to-be was the epitome of Christ's love for me. I had a reassurance that Bryan was the one I was supposed to marry based on God's love and his actions. Again, we don't profess to get it right all of the time and that we don't

75

go through times of selfishness. You can see that in our Mojave Desert Kerfuffle. However today, we do our best to work through them quickly, always looking to get back on the path to friendship and love.

It's a Choice

We all have a choice in determining if our marriage will veer off course, remain immobile in a dry arid place, or go the distance. We can choose to work towards an emotionally satisfying and fulfilling marriage based on the decisions we make every day. You may be wondering; how do I start? Counseling is always a beneficial option. Speaking to a trained professional or mature mentors with the skills to help you navigate honest and critical conversations is invaluable and has saved countless marriages, including ours. Other times, all it takes are small, consistent adjustments to make a significant impact. You can turbo-boost your marriage today by:

- **Comprising** – Ask yourself: *How can we both win in this situation?*
- **Valuing your spouse** – Ask yourself: *How can I show my spouse I value him or her?*
- **Being empathic** – Ask yourself: *How would I feel if the shoe were on the other foot?*
- **Listening to understand** – Ask yourself: *Am I listening to understand or waiting to tell my side?*
- **Making time for your spouse** – Ask yourself: *How am I showing my spouse they are a priority?*
- **Putting your spouse's needs first** – Ask your spouse: *Is there anything I can do for you?*

The benefits of making these small adjustments are endless. As you commit to asking yourself and your spouse these questions, you open the door for greater levels of friendship, communication, and intimacy, both emotional and physical. You don't have to wait; begin today and see the benefits.

YOUR STORY

Again we understand; this may be a challenging chapter. However, our goal is to create for you a clear and direct path to love. Before we go on to the next section, take a few moments to answer the questions below.

Questions to ask yourself (Not your spouse)

1. Are there times when I am selfish? How?

2. In what areas can I show my spouse I am looking out for their best interest?

Questions to ask your spouse

1. When I have acted selfishly in the past, how did it make you feel?

---

2. How can we tell each other when one is behaving selfishly in a way that won't lead to an argument? (A signal? A statement? Saying what you need specifically?)

_____

3. Are there healthy boundaries we need to establish for our marriage? If so, what are they and how do we begin and maintain them?

_____

_____

_____

_____

_____

_____

_____

HOMEWORK CHALLENGE #4

Temperature Checks

Incorporate a weekly or monthly "check-in" with your spouse. The goal of your relationship check-in is to see where you are, where you're going, and how you'd like to get there. Begin by establishing a regularly scheduled monthly check-in that works best for you and your spouse. The first of the month may be ideal so that you can review the past month. Once you get into the habit of doing it regularly, this will become natural and will develop organically. Establish a time with minimal or no interruptions. If you have small children, choose a time when the kids may be preoccupied, away, or sleeping.

Create a mini agenda. Jot down a few discussion points you'd like to share on paper or on your phone. Don't forget to pull out your calendar. Before you begin, establish a few ground rules, such as committing not to get angry or offended when your spouse shares their feelings or thoughts. Try to listen more than you speak. There are no right or wrong answers during your check-in, so stay solution-focused. The goal is to bring you closer, make adjustments where needed, and allow you both to be on the same page. You're a team; you got this! Below are a few examples and questions to help you get started.

Weekly or Monthly Check-Ins: Always start your conversation with wins and what went well.

✓ **Fun**

◉ What would you like to do this month/week together?

◉ Is there something we haven't done in a while that you'd like to do?

✓ **Appreciation**

◉ I appreciated it when you…

◉ I see the hard work you're putting into…

✓ **Connection**

◉ Are you feeling close to me?

◉ Do you need more physical intimacy?

✓ **Helping**

◉ How could we have done better with…?

◉ What are some things we need to work on this month/week?

Did you do the homework Challenge?

If you did, now's the time to reward yourselves. Do something that makes you and your spouse feel connected. Get creative!

We commit to rewarding ourselves by:

You're both on the right track! The temperature should feel just about right after that temperature check! Slow and steady wins the race. You're doing a great job fine tuning and providing maintenance to important areas within your marriage. Let's move on and find those U-turns so that we're headed toward the road to romance. We're almost there! You've got this!

Chapter Five

Forgiveness: The Road To Reconciliation

*I*n his poem, "An Essay of Criticism," Poet Alexander Pope wrote: "To err is human and to forgive is divine." By the sheer nature of our humanity, we will need to be forgiven at some point in our relationship, and if we desire to move forward in the relationship, we will also be required to forgive. Forgiveness is unavoidable in marriage and it may require divine assistance and the ability to tap into deeper depths within ourselves to accomplish it. It is inevitable, at some point spouses will miscommunicate, not always meet each other's expectations, and unfortunately will disappoint. It is a part of the human experience but can be overcome if we are willing to go through the process.

The healing process of forgiveness and the root causes of unforgiveness can be extremely complex, so we'll first begin by defining what forgiveness is not.

Forgiveness Is Not:

- A feeling
- Blind trust
- Always resolved quickly
- Condoning what was done
- The removal of consequences
- A cure that causes you to forget

We should also note that although God wants us to forgive, we do not believe nor does the bible condone any form of abuse in a relationship. There are no instances where we feel abuse of any kind, be it physical, mental, emotional, or financial, is justifiable. Abuse was never intended to be a part of God's plan for marriage. God loves and created marriage, but He loves the individuals within the marriage even more.

"Don't use foul or abusive language. Let everything you say be good and helpful, so that your words will be an encouragement to those who hear them. And do not bring sorrow to God's Holy Spirit by the way you live. Remember, he has identified you as his own, guaranteeing that you will be saved on the day of redemption. Get rid of all bitterness, rage, anger, harsh words, and slander, as well as all types of evil behavior. Instead, be kind to each other, tenderhearted, forgiving one another, just as God through Christ has forgiven you."

Ephesians 4:29-32 (NLT)

What Is Forgiveness?

If you look on the internet or read books by many notable experts, you'll find countless definitions, but forgiveness is simply...

The act of deciding to give up the right to get even or seek vengeance in order to free oneself from being emotionally enslaved to resentment, the pain of the jury, and the person who caused it.

If we're honest with ourselves, forgiveness can be extremely difficult. It can take days, weeks, months, and even years to forgive if we have not gone through the entire healing process. This is especially true if disappointments are consistent and cyclical. In some instances, it's not what the person did or said that caused the greatest injury; it's the disappointment and fear that the actions and behaviors that caused the initial injury will be repeated.

Why Is It So Hard to Forgive?

There are a number of reasons why we find it difficult to forgive. Some personality types find it challenging to forgive quickly. Others believe they can only forgive if the offender apologizes and makes restitution for what they have done. However, the most common reason we fail to or find it difficult to forgive is we believe that if we do forgive, we are letting the person who hurt us off the hook. This ultimately makes us believe that forgiveness only benefits the one who caused the pain, rather than the one who felt injured.

Many times, our natural tendency is to want to feel vindicated, see spontaneous changes in behavior, or a repentant heart take place. These terms and conditions may not occur right away, so we must be prepared to forgive even though this may not occur at all. As we shared, forgiveness is not condoning or allowing the hurt to continue; nor does it remove consequences. However, the focus is the transformation that occurs within our own hearts and minds.

Little Things Turn into Big Things

It's the "little things." A word spoken too flippantly, failing to consider the other person's feelings, and misinterpreting the other's motives were big for us. We assumed the other was not as forthcoming, so we questioned each other incessantly. These little instances caused an invisible chasm of distrust to develop in our relationship and we didn't realize it until it was almost too late. We discovered after dealing with the same issues year after year, the root cause of many of our problems were unresolved issues from our childhood; and it took a great deal of time, soul searching, healing, and perseverance to resolve. We were forced to confront the issues that caused us to think and behave the way that we did. We were at a crossroads and knew we had to make a decision about the future of our marriage. Deciding we wanted to stay in the marriage, the first decision we made was to forgive each other, work towards forgetting about the past, and learn how to focus on the future.

Reasons to Forgive

Although forgiveness can be difficult, it is necessary. Studies have shown that failing to forgive can negatively impact our mental, physical, and emotional well-being. It places the body in a flight-or-fight mode causing elevated blood pressure, increased anxiety, high stress levels, and in some instances, depression. Not only does it negatively impact our health, failing to forgive prevents us from moving forward with the relationship and on to the healing process.

Although forgiveness helps us physically, mentally, and emotionally, the most important reason we should forgive is because God calls for us to do so.

"Bear with each other and forgive whatever grievances you may have against one another. Forgive as the Lord forgave you."

Colossians 3:13 (NIV)

"Get rid of all bitterness, rage, and anger, brawling and slander, along with every form of malice. Be kind and compassionate to one another, forgiving each other, just as in Christ God forgave you."

Ephesians 4:31–32 (NIV)

"And when you stand praying, if you hold anything against anyone, forgive him, so that your Father in heaven may forgive you your sins."

Mark 11:25 (NIV)

Simply, we have been extended the grace of forgiveness. Jesus understood betrayal, disappointment, and pain beyond what we could ever imagine, yet He still forgave. He is the perfect example of the ability to forgive, and He gives us the divine ability to do so if we are truly willing. Since forgiveness is first and foremost about us and a gift we give ourselves, we grant it so that we are no longer enslaved and tethered to the past. We do not have to continue to relive painful moments as if a bungee cord were tied around our ankles, yanking us back to the moment of grief, anger, or disappointment. We can decide to untie ourselves, move forward, and heal. However, this will take intentionality and discipline.

It Starts with the Mind: You Can Reroute Your Thoughts

We have the ability to refocus, reroute, and replace negative thoughts; doing this can help bring us back into focus and see the light at the end of the tunnel. When your brain attempts to take you down this road, consciously take an inventory of your thoughts, and replace them with new ones. The following passages below gives you a good example of what you can replace those thoughts with.

"Summing it all up, friends, I'd say you'll do best by filling your minds and meditating on things true, noble, reputable, authentic, compelling, gracious, the best, not the worst; the beautiful, not the ugly; things to praise, not things to curse. Put into practice what you learned from me, what you heard and saw and realized. Do that, and God, who makes everything work together, will work you into his most excellent harmonies."

Philippians 4:8–9 (MSG)

"We take captive every thought to make it obedient to Christ."

2 Corinthians 10:5b (NIV)

Take negative thoughts captive and replace them with scriptures that encourage you. You don't have to allow your thoughts to escape like a runaway train, you *can* control your thoughts. Let us show you, try this quick exercise: Begin thinking about a vacation destination you've taken or one you'd like to take. Think about it for10-20 seconds, then begin reciting in your mind the multiplication table beginning with multiples of 7. (Ex.7x1=7, 7x2=14 etc.) You interrupted your thoughts of the vacation when you began multiplying; notice it was pretty tough trying to think of two things simultaneously. That's what the scripture 2 Corinthians 10:5 wants you to. Change your thought pattern. When you change your thoughts you transform your thinking, mood and emotions because feelings always follow thoughts. When you meditate and put into practice thinking on things that uplift you, it will bring a sense of rest to your mind.

Another way to begin rerouting your thoughts and managing your emotions is to do something you enjoy. Focus on things that bring you fulfillment and joy, diverting your attention from the negative situation. Begin focusing on people, places, and things that personally make you happy. It could be going to dinner with a friend, writing, trying a new hobby, going for a walk, or playing your favorite video game. Doing things you enjoy creates positive emotions allowing you to see clearly and from a different perspective.

How to Forgive When It's Hard

We've gone over a few reasons why it may be hard to forgive, the reasons why we should, and the benefits of forgiving, but how do we do it when we feel we can't or that our spouse doesn't necessarily "deserve" it?

1. Discuss

Discuss it with God first. Tell Him how you feel. 1 Peter 5:7 says, give all your worries and cares to God, for He cares about you. You'll notice the first thing He wants us to do is give Him all of the things that hurt and worry us because He cares. When you give Him those things, you are saying God; I know you care about me and what concerns me. So leave it in His hands and ask Him to heal the hurt, help you to forgive, and give you the peace and wisdom to move forward.

When the time is right, you should also discuss what caused you to feel hurt or disappointed with your spouse. Be specific about how their actions hurt you in order to give you both an opportunity to work though the issue. For example: "I felt embarrassed when you raised your voice in front of..." Also, be specific about future expectations and if needed, incorporate boundaries that may need to be put in place moving forward.

2. Decide

Decide you will not allow unforgiveness to enslave you by letting go of the bitterness, resentment, and the need to avenge yourself. There are times when we have to decide if something warrants our time, attention, or response. Slight annoyances can be resolved relatively quickly and the way we feel about them doesn't have to be drawn out for hours or days. Pick your battles, decide what can be negotiated, and address issues that have the potential to negatively impact your relationship.

3. Do

Do what it takes to protect your thoughts and be aware of negative self-talk. Our brains are wired to remember events, especially if there is an emotion tied to them. Our feelings can change instantly, so don't allow them to control you or make decisions that may have a long term, negative impact on your friendship and marriage.

Seeking Forgiveness

When a spouse extends forgiveness, it does not give the spouse who caused the injury a license to continue the behavior that negatively impacted the marriage. The ultimate goal is to maintain the friendship, regain the feeling of love, and stay on the same road preventing either spouse from heading to the nearest exit.

However, negative behaviors or repeated actions over time can result in negative consequences. So let's take a few moments to inspect your C. A. R to make sure you are heading in the right direction and on the road to reconciliation.

If you determine you have inadvertently caused your spouse pain, use our C.A.R.S. Method to get your relationship back on track.

C – Course correct without justifying your actions. Sometimes you have to go further than just saying, "I'm sorry." If we say we're sorry and fail to correct our actions, our spouse may believe that our apology was not sincere, disingenuous, and may not believe the integrity of your apology the next time you apologize.

A – Acknowledge and accept your role. This is not an apology; this is merely expressing empathy. Cleary share how your actions may have hurt them. Your spouse simply wants you to acknowledge that you understand why they feel hurt or upset.

R – Right the wrong. This may be the most challenging. Ask if there is something you can do to make it right. Change an action? Behavior? Response? Don't view this type of vulnerability as giving up control. Focus on the healing that takes place as you both work to resolve the issue.

S –Say you are sorry and that you are committed to not hurting them again. Ultimately your spouse not only wants to believe that your apology is sincere, they also want to be assured of your love and willingness to protect the relationship.

Forgive Yourself

If the hurt you caused your spouse still plagues you after you've committed to moving forward, there's one more person you have to forgive, and that's yourself. Although forgiveness is not about forgetting, it is about letting go of the past so that you can move toward and reestablish a new path for your marriage. You cannot change what happened; but you can change your actions moving forward and that's what counts. The process of healing may take a while. Still, it can be done. If you are on a spiritual journey and feel your actions have impacted your relationship with God, go to Him and ask for forgiveness; He loves you unconditionally. It may be difficult at times to ask to be forgiven, but God is always willing to forgive a repentant heart. Forgive yourself and head toward your healing.

"The Lord is compassionate and gracious, slow to anger, abounding in love. He will not always accuse, nor will he harbor his anger forever; he does not treat us as our sins deserve or repay us according to our iniquities. For as high as the heavens are above the earth, so great is his love for those who fear him; as far as the east is from the west, so far has he removed our transgressions from us."

Psalm 103:8–12 (NIV)

YOUR STORY

Your spouse not only has a love language they have an apology language as well. Taking the apology language quiz will allow you to discover what your spouse feels is a sincerely genuine apology. When you know what truly touches your spouse's heart when you apologize, you can renew your love relationship and grow stronger in your marriage.

Go to the 5 Love Languages website at: 5lovelanguages.com Under the "Quizzes" link, take Dr Gary Chapman's "Apology Quiz."

1. What is your apology language?

_____

2. What is your spouse's apology language?

_____

Take a few moments to discuss your spouse's love and apology language

3. How can you show your spouse your apology is sincere?

_____

_____

4. What can you do this week to make your spouse feel loved?

_____

_____

HOMEWORK CHALLENGE #5

Language of Love

Write an electronic or paper "I am Sincerely Sorry" list. Each spouse should list ten things they are deeply sorry they said, did that hurt their spouse, or something they sincerely regret. Taking turns, starting at the top of the list, say, "I am sincerely sorry for…" Be sure to make eye contact while sharing. After the lists are read, accept your spouse's sincere apology and commit to moving forward.

Did you complete the questions and homework challenge?

Did you discover your love and apology language? Did you write your Sincerely Sorry list? All right! Now is the time to reward yourselves for a job well done. Do something this week that speaks your spouse's love language. Make it a habit and commit to doing something small every day!

We commit to rewarding ourselves by:

Good job making that U-turn! You're headed in the right direction! Since you've been driving for a while, take a few moments to refresh yourselves and get some well-deserved rest.

Chapter Six

Self-Care Is Not Selfish

On an extended road trip, you may be tempted to drive a few extra hours to get to your destination as quickly as possible, but disregarding your need to rest periodically could prove to be dangerous down the road. It may feel inconvenient however, taking those few extra moments to pull over to the nearest rest stop or service station can prove to be invaluable to you, your spouse, and your family in the long run.

Similar to going on a long arduous journey, failing to make self-care a priority in marriage can leave us running on fumes, mentally, physically, and emotionally if we fail to stop and rest from time to time. This is certainly easier said than done when we face what seems to be insurmountable responsibilities related to family, work, and business. These obligations require not only a great deal of our time but our energy as well. So much so, if we are not careful, we can find ourselves unable to give our best selves to the people we care about the most.

Self-Care and The "Oxygen Mask Rule"

Self-care is anything you do for yourself that helps you take care of your mental, emotional, and physical well-being. It is also about knowing yourself well enough to recognize when you are running low on energy and taking the time to refuel, rather than letting yourself run on empty. Self-care is not a luxury or reward you give yourself from time to time by simply going to the spa, getting a detox body wrap, or an hour-long hot stone massage. These one-off activities can and do, offer temporary relief from stress; but don't offer long-term solutions that get to the root issues that caused you to initially seek out the services. These root causes stem from both internal and external factors that must be addressed if we want to live the life we desire.

In chapter four, we discussed the damaging effects of selfishness in a marriage. By definition, selfishness is solely concerned with one's own needs while not considering the needs of others. However, the "self" in self-care is not selfish. If you have ever flown on an airplane, you've most certainly heard the attendant make the following announcement: "Should the cabin lose pressure, oxygen masks will drop from the overhead compartment; place the mask over your mouth first before assisting others." Are they asking us to be selfish by placing our mask on first in that instance? No, because they understand that passengers can quickly lose consciousness when the cabin pressure is dangerously low on oxygen. So their goal is to ensure that once your oxygen mask is on first, you will then have the ability to help those you love or those closest to you. That should be the goal when thinking about self-care; to take care of yourself so that you have the mental and emotional energy to enjoy your life and be there for those most important to you.

Running low on oxygen looks very much like burnout when we push ourselves to utter exhaustion or until we completely give out. So how do you know when you are reaching that point of exhaustion? Very similar to the blaring red light on a car's dashboard, our bodies and minds send us signals when we are out of alignment and in need of a break.

Running on Fumes

There are a number of signs and symptoms that indicate you may be running on empty because you have not made self-care a priority:

1. You are on autopilot
2. Easily angered or moody
3. Feeling lonely or isolated
4. Skipping meals or overeating
5. Neglectful of family and friends
6. Experiencing fatigued-related insomnia
7. Feeling resentful because of a lack of rest
8. Feeling obligated to take care of everyone and everything

Reasons Why We Don't Make Self-Care a Priority

If you ask the average person why they don't make time for themselves and focus on self-care, you will usually hear:

- "I don't have time"
- "I don't have support"
- "I'll get to it eventually"
- "I don't know where to start"
- "I don't have enough energy"
- "Who's going to do it if I don't?"
- "It's my job, this is what I signed up for"

Those are all very legitimate reasons; however, there are three other common factors that prevent us from focusing on self-care that we may not realize or readily admit. These external factors and stressors impact our ability to truly make it a part of our daily and weekly lifestyle.

1. Guilt

We can begin to feel guilt-ridden when we don't have a proper perspective of self-care; and may falsely believe that if we make ourselves a priority, our family will feel neglected as a result. Don't misunderstand us; we don't want you to drain the bank and run off to Tahiti (although that may sound tempting on a challenging day.) Taking a few minutes to an hour daily to do something that benefits your well-being is beneficial for both you and your family. Parents, particularly mothers, have a difficult time taking off their Wonder Woman cape, which is something they have definitely earned! However, Wonder Woman AKA Diana Prince, did take time off once in a while to go on a few dates with Steve Trevor! We have the proof on our Limited Edition DVD collection!

Self-care is not a zero sum game that says you take away from your children or spouse when you do something for yourself. You will actually be giving them the gift of your best self when you have more energy, are feeling less stress, and have the ability to focus on what's important. This is not only a win for your family but a win for you. Stop feeling guilty, you are important to your family as well as your relationship; begin seeing yourself from that perspective.

"Am I now trying to win the approval of human beings, or of God? Or am I trying to please people? If I were still trying to please people, I would not be a servant of Christ."

Galatians 1:10 (NIV)

"Fearing people is a dangerous trap, but trusting the LORD means safety."

Proverbs 29:25 (NLT)

---

2. People Pleasing

Self-care can be challenging if you have a difficult time saying no. We all have at one point in our lives fallen into the trap of desiring to please people or have overcommitted ourselves because we wanted to help someone only to regret it later. You are not a genie in a bottle placed on earth to grant everyone's wish. You were meant to live out your life the way God intended with a great sense of freedom, purpose, and love. It's okay to say no. It may sound negative but there is a positive in it.

When you are saying no, you are really saying yes to something else. Yes, to a date with your spouse, yes to an outing with your children, or yes to some much-needed time alone to rejuvenate for the next challenge you have to tackle. Those who love and respect you will honor your "no" or "not right now." Having a hard time saying no? It's all in the language. Some people are very good at saying no because they have practiced building up their "no muscle." Just in case you are still building yours up, we have developed scenarios and talking points that will be helpful starting out.

Strengthen Your "No Muscle" and Say Yes to Self-Care

At one point in our marriage, we were burned out; the stress on our jobs was at an all-time high, and we were overcommitted in almost every area of our life. We were hanging on by a thread and knew that we were destined to crash and burn if we didn't stop while we were ahead. We didn't want to hurt the feelings of those we loved, but we were desperate for a change. However, at the time we didn't know how to say no.

We knew it wouldn't be easy at first, so we began practicing and scripting our responses to help prepare ourselves for counter-responses, which we knew we'd receive a lot of. "We need you," "They need you," "Well, what about..?" came at us from all sides, but we held the line and said 'yes' to our peace, sanity, and marriage. We were so used to saying yes and found it difficult to fight through the barrage of guilt, but eventually, it became easier. We strengthened our "no muscle" so that we could focus on our marriage and emotional needs.

Below are a few examples we used and encourage others to use, as a way to say yes to self-care and bring balance back into their lives.

1. If you don't have time you can say:

- "I'm sorry, but I have a prior commitment."

- "Unfortunately, I won't be able to help out this time. However, I'm available on __ (day) at ___(time)."

- "I have a long-standing commitment and I'm not available for the next few days/weeks."

- "I'm sorry, I won't be able to commit to that (project, event, or committee) right now; my hands are full."

- "I would have loved to help, but I can't at this time. Check back with me in the Spring/Summer." (If you'd like to participate later)

2. Add a boundary if you have time in your schedule. You can say:

- "I have a few commitments that I need to take care of, but I am available on ___ (day) at ___(time) or if that doesn't work, I'm also available on __ (day) at ___(time)."

Wanting to help is admirable, but things that are "good" should be screened through your self-care test. Before committing, ask yourself, Do I have time for this? Will it take me off course? Have I planned for this? What will happen if I say yes? Can I do this next week? Don't be afraid to let people know you are locked into a previous commitment. Those previous commitments are the things you have prioritized for yourself and your family.

3.Control Freaks-R-US

We pride ourselves in self-sufficiency, but deep down inside, we really do desire assistance when times get a little stressful. Our problem? The control freak in us. We are sometimes afraid to let go and take the needed time for self-care because we're afraid that if we don't do "X", it won't be done "right." We want to forgo the feeling of aggravation if it's not done correctly or the way we think it should be done; and justify it by saying, "I should do it because it won't be done quickly," "I don't want to have to clean up after your volunteerism" or "It's just easier if I do it."

If your spouse asks to take a few things off of your plate, do you sometimes refuse their help because you're afraid they won't do it your way? If that's the case, you are inadvertently sabotaging your self-care. If your spouse wants to cook, do the dishes (well, load the dishwasher), and put the kids to bed, allow them to do so. When they cook, yes, they may cook the meal on high or put a bit too much or not enough seasoning in the food. The dishwasher may not be aligned perfectly with the plates on the bottom and cups on the top. The kids may still have a bit of sauce on their face even after their bath; it's okay. No one will die. What will happen is you will have a few moments of peace and much-needed rest.

Remember, if your spouse is offering to support you when you need it, it is not their intention to do it all wrong; they are just doing it differently. You may be thinking, what if I let them do it, won't I ultimately have to go behind them and do it again? No, maybe not all of it. Go ahead and take a chill pill and remember no one died in the process-that's success in our book! You received the rest you needed, your spouse feels like they saved the day and was an important part of the team; and that is a win for everyone.

You may have grown up in a house that encouraged self-reliance, to push through until the end or avoid sharing your need for assistance. Remember, your spouse may not have grown up that way. Support looks different to everyone, so if they offer support, allow them to help.

Benefits of Making Self-Care a Priority

The benefits of self-care outweigh the reasons why we believe we cannot make it a part of our daily lives. There are 24 hours in a day, so we owe it to ourselves to carve out time to take care of our mental, physical, and emotional needs. It's okay to check in with yourself periodically to see what your mind and body requires. There are no rules when it comes to self-care; just taking small steps daily can make a world of difference. Everyone's self-care routine will be different; you just have to discover what helps you feel refreshed, rejuvenated, and fulfilled.

Self-care is much more than a desire to feel good. It is a commitment you make to yourself that increases your chance of being around a lot longer to experience the things you dream of doing during your lifetime. Getting a good night's sleep, having a well-rested mind, and the energy to focus on your marriage's physical and emotional needs are only a few benefits of self-care.

Self-Care Ideas You Can Start Today

We have provided you with a few mental, physical, emotional, and spiritual self-care activities you can start doing today. Remember, these are only suggestions. Only you know what works best for you and what makes you feel rested and rejuvenated. Whether all or only a few of the ideas in the list below will work for you, the goal is to begin intentionally and consistently.

4 WAYS TO BEGIN PRACTICING
SELF-CARE TODAY

Emotional Self-Care

- Delegate a task
- Practice saying no
- Journal your feelings
- Schedule in "me time"
- Practice asking for help
- Begin to set small boundaries
- Call and talk to a close friend
- Seek out a healthy support system
- Watch a movie that makes you laugh
- Buy an essential oil diffuser and try using aromatherapy essential oils

Mental Self-Care

- Do something creative
- Take a technology break
- Try something you've never done
- Avoid or reduce time with toxic people
- Write out and meditate on inspirational affirmations
- Travel to an area, restaurant, or state you've never visited
- Write a list of 10 things that you are grateful for and review them daily
- Listen to a podcast on a topic that interests you, one you have yet to explore.
- Take a fun virtual tour around the world (YouTube: Wanderlust Travel Videos)

Physical Self-Care

- Exercise
- Try a new hairstyle
- Rearrange your furniture
- Declutter a space that bothers you
- Cuddle up with someone you love
- Start an indoor or outdoor garden
- Take a virtual or in-person dance class
- Take a virtual or in-person exercise class
- Do an indoor or outdoor activity you enjoy

Spiritual Self-Care

- Ask a friend to pray with you
- Read the bible or a book that inspires you
- Watch an inspirational sermon or podcast
- Listen to worship, soaking or uplifting songs
- Spend time in prayer (Talk to God about how you feel)
- Read scriptures and passages that speaks of God's love for you (Ex. Jeremiah 31:3)
- Join a spiritually supportive virtual or in-person small group community

There Is Only One You

There is only one you and those who love you want to see, experience, and spend time with the best you for years to come. To expect you or your spouse to run at 100 miles per hour consistently without taking time to refuel and refocus is unrealistic. When you build a lifestyle of self-care, you have the time and energy to build a trusting and supportive relationship. As a result, you will see the intimacy and friendship grow in your marriage exponentially. That is definitely the making of a recipe and lifestyle of romance. Now that you are are committed to taking time to rejuvenate, refocus and refresh, let's put into practice what you've learned and then move on to the next chapter, destination romance!

YOUR STORY

Use the list provided to begin your lifestyle of self-care. Pick one from each chart that works best for you. As you practice self-care, you can't forget about your spouse. You should also focus on "pair care" and take turns taking care of each other.

Step 1

Make a list of ideas for your personalized self-care routine. Make sure the list is realistic and attainable. If you need ideas use the list provided in the previous page. If you're having trouble thinking of ideas that are tailor-made for you that are not listed, try asking and completing the following sentences:

- I feel fulfilled and rested when I have the time to

_____ and _____

- I feel frustrated when I don't have the time to

_____ and _____

Step 2

Decide which of these self-care routines can be feasibly done on a daily, weekly or monthly basis. Make sure you can implement them. This increases the likelihood of your success.

HOMEWORK CHALLENGE #6

Pair Care Check-In

On a daily basis ask yourself as well as your spouse the following questions:

1) How are you feeling today?

2) What do you need today?

3) What boundaries do you need to establish or reinforce today?

4) Did you have an opportunity to practice self-care today? Yesterday?

Go beyond asking, "How was your day?" Be sure to ask specific questions focusing on the current physical, mental, emotional, and even spiritual space your spouse may be in. Doing this together ensures you are giving, as well as receiving support from each other. Allow your spouse to support you and don't be afraid to be vulnerable. One spouse may be strong one day and the other the next. This is how love, trust, and camaraderie are infused into your relationship.

Did you complete the questions and homework challenge?

If you did, then you and your spouse should reward yourselves. Do something to pamper yourselves. Use your answer from step 1 as your starting point.

We commit to rewarding ourselves by:

You've learned the importance of self-care and the benefits of getting rest. When you take care of yourself, you have energy to take care of one another. Let's use that energy to start a fire in the next chapter!

Chapter Seven

Rekindling the Romance

Fan the Flames

*T*aking a road trip across the country, you will find there are many picturesque places where you can stop, rest, stretch your legs, and admire nature's beauty. A good way to do that is by stopping at beautifully wooded campsite along the way. We're only a few miles away from destination romance, so let's park here for a few moments, start a small fire, chat, and then we'll be on our way.

Have you ever been warmed by a fire on a cold day? The flickering red embers and sound of crackling wood brings warmth to your body and your heart, especially when you're with the one you love. After a while, what begins to happen when the flame dies down? You gradually feel the coolness of the night air that was once at bay suddenly begin to envelop you. You grab the nearest sweater or blanket to retain the heat because the warmth you previously felt begins to dissipate.

Romance in a marriage can be much like a fire that slowly dwindles over time. As day to day routines are established, couples may find themselves in a rut discovering one day the flames that once burned bright are dimming and all that is left are little glowing embers. Before long, they may begin wondering *how did the fire of our romance burn out?* The short answer is, any flame will slowly wane when left unchecked.

Signs your romance flame has waned:

- Date night is a distant memory

- You only talk about business or the kids

- You're having the same fight over and over again

- You are having little to no sex and avoiding intimacy

- You've become bored and disinterested in each other

- You can't remember the last time you kissed or cuddled

- Your phone or computer gets more attention than your spouse

Experienced campers know the art of building and maintaining a fire, so we'll take a few pages out of their 'fire starter 101' handbook to learn how to start and maintain those marriage flames again. Starting a bonfire is pretty easy however, maintaining it is a bit more complicated. When starting a fire, you need three essential elements fuel, oxygen and a flame. Your fuel will consist of your kindling, usually small sticks and wood to keep the fire going. Of course, you can't forget about the flame to get the fire started. Once burning, you can continue to add small amounts of kindling being careful not to smother it. There are a number of things that can smother the flame of romance if we're not paying close enough attention. Selfishness, busyness, complacency, and being overly argumentative are just a few things that can smother your flames, causing feelings of love and romance to wane. If you're beginning to feel a chill or little to no heat in the area of romance, start by asking yourself as well as your spouse four simple questions.

1. *What caused our fire to wane?*

2. *Did life logs smother our feelings of intimacy?*

3. *What can we do to begin reigniting our love flames again?*

4. *Is our flame smoldering with just a few embers or has it completely burned out?*

All flames need oxygen to burn. However, if the flame is deprived of oxygen it will eventually go out or become smothered under the weight of large logs. Are there major life logs that have smothered your flames? These logs are major life issues we don't anticipate early on in marriage; illness, fatigue, financial difficulties, stress, and external commitments can all weigh a couple down over time.

The buildup of ash is another factor that can smother the flame in your marriage. Failing to deal with past issues that have not been resolved can cause a spouse to fume in silence. However, where there is ash there is always hope. Hope *can* arise from the ashes if there are still embers hidden within. These small flickers of hope give you an indication that there is still life and the potential of burning bright again, but you have to stoke the flames again.

Stoking the Flames

Stoking a fire is an art and the wood must be shifted just right to maintain maximum heat. This ensures the pieces of wood are close enough to feed on one another's heat to maintain the blaze. It is not enough to stoke the flames occasionally; you must be sure to tend to it regularly to ensure the flame does not go out. Have you ever noticed a piece of firewood fall quite a distance away from a fire? What normally happens? It usually stops burning, right? That's because the wood needs to be close enough to the other embers in order to burn. The further it is away from its heat source, the more the air cools it and causes the fire to go out more quickly. The closer you are to your heat source (your spouse) throughout life challenges, the harder it will be to separate you from the warmth of each other's love.

You must become a master stoker because you are the architect of your flame. If you don't know where to begin, find other couples who are on fire and passionate about their marriage to help you get fired up again. Remember, if your fire is low and embers are present, there is still hope. It was a slow process to reach that point, so it may be a slow process to build up the blaze again, and that's okay. Nurture your flame with the new kindling and stoke it until you see a blaze again.

Fanning the Flame

We discovered one day that our once wildfire romance had dwindled down to only a few mere embers. This was an unseasonably cold winter in our marriage, and we inadvertently found ourselves becoming roommates. We were like ships passing in the night and living our own separate lives; one would come in from an overnight shift, while the other would be headed off to work. There was no time or desire for any form of intimacy, we weren't even friends "with benefits." After a while, we found ourselves not being physically intimate for days at a time. Days turned into weeks and weeks turned into months without having any form of intimacy. This subsequently changed the dynamic of the relationship. The embers grew cold because we were not connecting meaningfully, both physically and emotionally. We had different expectations, wants and desires, and neither of our needs were being met. This tension pulled us further apart, and we knew we had to rebuild a more intimate connection emotionally before we could connect physically again. Being vulnerable and sharing with your spouse how you feel about aspects of your intimate life or the lack thereof, can be quite stressful if you've avoided it for some time. Fearful that an argument might ensue or that the other person would feel they were being blamed for the state of the marriage, we suffered in silence. However, we knew we had to rip the band-aid off and place everything on the table in a transparent, yet gracious way. Eventually and very tactfully, we discussed what we needed from each other, temptations we faced as a result of not connecting physically, and the loneliness we felt being apart. We faced the issues head on and slowly worked our way to rebuilding a sense of closeness and intimacy again.

Begin with intimacy

Intimacy is the feeling of safety and closeness you have towards your spouse and is built on kindness, appreciation, affection, attention, quality time, physical touch, and gracious communication. We focused on intimacy and found little ways to reestablish our connection; and through those little things, we reignited a spark. We discovered although the physical act of intimacy is certainly important, it is not the most important aspect of the relationship. It is all of the things that lead up to it that makes a stronger connection both emotionally and sexually.

Intimacy begins with nonsexual touching and is a powerful way to affirm love and foster a sense of closeness. It also requires giving them your undivided attention, so begin with focusing on your spouse, intimate touch; and see where it leads because the ultimate goal is connection. Here are a few ways to ensure the fire stays burning bright in your marriage. These methods are tried and true.

Let's start with a little kindling for your fire:

- Give a lingering kiss

- Go to bed at the same time

- While hugging caress your spouse's lower back

- Sit close enough so that your legs and arms are touching

- Look into their eyes; let them know they have your undivided attention

- Before you fall asleep express gratitude for one thing your spouse did that day

- Give each other a ten-minute massage before going to bed using aromatic powders or oils

- Make love using your words telling your spouse how attracted you are to them and how attractive they are to you

- Use your voice, tell your spouse what you liked or enjoyed. You can say "I liked it when you___."

- Focus on the sensation of touch, gently touch their shoulders, neck, fingers, ears, legs and face. Focus on the sensation of being the receiver and the giver

- Make your bedroom conducive to intimacy and rest by taking the television out of your bedroom. It will feel awkward at first, but it is a game changer

Creating intimacy outside of the bedroom will create a meaningful connection inside the bedroom. Physical touch like caressing, hugging, and kissing activate receptors in our skin that stimulate our brains to produce oxytocin, the bonding hormone. Remember, our bodies were created to give and receive love, so begin practicing these techniques to fan the flames of romance. Embers *can* produce flames under the right conditions when you're committed to doing it together. Keep adding your love kindling and watch those sparks fly.

YOUR STORY

You may be doing well in this area of keeping the fire ablaze in your marriage; if so, keep it going! If you are working on stoking your flames, great job, keep on stoking! Below are a few activities you can do together. The next chapter, Destination: Romance will be sure to add more heat to your marital fire, so let's get going!

Answer the following questions based on the flame-to-wane section above. Choose two areas you are doing well in and two where you would like to improve.

1) Is date night a distant memory?

_____

• When was the last time you went on a date? Where did you go?

_____

2) Are you having little to no sex and avoiding intimacy?

_____

- If so, why?

_____

3) Have you become a little bored with your routine?

_____

- If so, what are some ways you both can change that?

_____

4) Does your phone or computer get more attention than your spouse?

_____

- If so, what can you both do to change that?

_____

5) When was the last time you discussed the intimate aspect of your relationship?

What was the outcome?

_____

6) What are some creative ways you can begin fanning the flames of romance in your marriage?

_____

_____

_____

_____

_____

HOMEWORK CHALLENGE #7

Focus on Affection

Begin with intimacy and focus on affection. Touch is a powerful way to connect to the one you love. Remember sharing meaningful touch with your spouse produces oxytocin the "bonding cuddle chemical" in the brain, causing us to feel more connected. Over the next two weeks, do one of the following "focus" or "touch" activities <u>every day.</u>

- Hold hands while talking
- Hug your spouse from behind
- Shut your phones off at a certain time in the evening
- Hold hands in bed before you fall asleep (our favorite)
- Share a lingering kiss (make is slow and make it count)
- Hold hands whenever you can when you are in public
- Intentionally remember the good qualities of your spouse

- Interrupt your routine by doing something small yet different
- Rearrange your bedroom furniture and freshen it up with new linen

Did you complete the questions and homework challenge?

If you did, remember to reward yourselves! Do something fun and flirtatious you haven't done in a while.

We commit to rewarding ourselves by:

_____

You started a fire in this chapter, let's look at ways to keep it ablaze in the next!

Chapter Eight

Destination: Romance

W elcome to the next stop on your romantic journey, it has been quite the ride! On the first leg of the journey, you picked up your communication keys, filled up your trust tank, navigated through a few detours and an extremely bumpy ride at times. In addition, you also had an opportunity to stop and take a much needed rest, go on a virtual tour around the world, and warm yourselves by a romantic fire. Job well done! There's still work to be done, but now is the time for fun! In this section, the goal is to be daringly creative and pull out all of the stops. As always, we are here just to offer a few suggestions that will provide you with a greater sense of anticipation, excitement, and fun as you prepare yourself for this romantic adventure ahead. So, let's get started!

1. Get Inside Your Spouse's Head

Are you a student of your spouse? What does he or she like? What excites them? What doesn't? What makes them feel loved, appreciated, sexy, needed, and wanted? Begin to take an inventory of all of these things so that you can begin "Operation Romance Full Speed Ahead." Remember, as you start this journey, make sure you include plans and activities that are tailor-made just for your spouse. You may not want to get too creative, especially in the beginning, if you know that your spouse is a bit particular when it pertains to certain things. For instance, if your spouse is not a fan of Smokey the Bear's Wilderness Adventures, it may not be a good idea to schedule a camping trip or picnic in the woods. Know your audience.

Also, keep in mind, we all change throughout our marriage. The wife, who once loved getting flowers during your engagement, may not prefer them now. She may want a spa day or a gadget that makes her life run more proficiently, and the new groom who loved collecting watches may now prefer a new video game or deluxe car wash and detail. As you begin becoming a student of your spouse, their curiosity may be piqued because of the questions you are subtly asking about their wants and needs. Use that to create anticipation for what you have planned for them. It's human nature to want to know what's going on, so use it to your advantage. If you have a spouse who does not like surprises, you can simply let them know you'd like to do something nice for them that you believe they'll enjoy. If you prefer a stealthier approach, ask questions over dinner related to something that you're planning, such as, "What do you think about___?" "How would you like to spend our anniversary/your birthday?" Their answers will usually give you an idea of their preferences.

2. Think About Them

The old adage "where your mind goes, your heart and body follows" is certainly true. Throughout the day, think about your spouse. Meditate on what you love about them and something they did for you that was unforgettable. When you begin remembering the love that you have for your spouse, you will begin to feel closer to them, and that love cocktail of dopamine in your brain will begin to activate. Remember, your mind is a supercomputer and it can heighten the emotions of love. Focus on what brings you joy about your spouse and relationship.

3. Plan Ahead

In order to make any date night successful, you'll need to ensure that both of your schedules are in sync. Check to see if they have anything pending on their calendar. Also, ensure they are at their best. Allow them an opportunity to wind down if they've had a long day. Also, be sure your plan is conducive to romance. Is the house free of clutter? Will there be distractions? Do you have reservations? Tickets? Make a checklist so there are no roadblocks to your well-laid plans.

Ready, Set, Go!

If you're unsure where to start, we have included a few date night ideas to get the party started! Remember, do what works best for you and your spouse in your current season of marriage. We have included some inexpensive dates that you can do both inside and outside of your home. You don't have to break the bank or spend $100 to have a good time! You can have fun and be frugal at the same time!

We discovered this when we went from earning six figures a year to just breaking even during a financial crisis in our life. During the financial crisis of 2008, one of the companies we were working for downsized and we found ourselves left with $35 at the end of the week after our bills were paid, so we certainly could not afford to splurge on anything. At that moment, we decided to get a little creative and appreciate the little things. We'd have date night at McDonald's at the end of each week and buy a $1 cheeseburger and an ice cream. If we had a surplus one week, we'd splurge and buy two small fries. This financial crisis and season in our marriage allowed us to work as a team, get to know each other better and become more creative in ways we'd never imagined. During that time let's just say we played a lot of Uno! Financial stress caused by external factors beyond your control, can either make you bitter or better; we chose the latter and you can do the same.

Destination Romance Date Nights Ideas

In this section, we are deputizing you as an official love mechanic because you alone have the power to fix, remove, add and replace things in your marriage that will strengthen it for years to come. We've added just a few ideas to help get you started.

1. Set the Atmosphere

Set the atmosphere by setting up a mini spa for your spouse. If you have a bathtub in your home run a bubble bath. Play nice music in the background. Light a few candles in the bathroom and don't forget the fragrant bath bombs. If you don't have a bathtub a nice foot spa will also work. You can use a portable foot spa or a fancy container will do. After your spouse has soaked their feet in bath salts, choose a nice lotion you know they will enjoy. You can then prop their feet up on your lap and massage them until their heart's content.

2. Express Yourself

Do you write? Sing? Play an instrument? Then the sky's the limit! Write a song, poem, or letter to your sweetheart showing them how much they mean to you. If you want to get even more creative use your camera to film yourself showing off those skills! This is a great memento they can look back on in the days, weeks, and years to come.

3. Finger Food Fridays

On a Friday night, set up a platter full of only finger foods. This night, your mission is to only feed each other. After feeding each other a while, it will get a little interesting...

4. Ask Your Spouse Again

Who doesn't want to feel like they've still "got it?" Well, you both do! Take turns asking each other out on a date again. Each spouse should take turns planning the surprise date. The mission here is to actually ask your spouse out on a formal date. Did you forget how to do it? Below you will find a few ideas from our very own play book.

- *"Hi, I'd like to take you out for coffee, does Tuesday work for you?"*

- *"Do you like seafood? I know a great restaurant that I think you might like near me. Can I pick you up at 7:00?"*

- *"What are your plans later this week? I found a nice spot with the best tapas, I'd love to take you there."*

We don't know about you, but that makes us giddy!

5. Choose a Themed In-Home Movie Night

We love culturally diverse foods, so here's a suggestion. Choose a culturally diverse movie and try to cook (or order in) a meal based on a common dish for that culture. We love Italian food, so we'll whip up a common Italian dish and watch an Italian themed movie. Immerse yourself in culture!

Operation Romance: Do it Day or Night

Here are a few more date night ideas that will spice things up and add a little bit of turbo boost to your romantic days or nights. No need to thank us, you're welcome!

1. Recreate your first date
2. Prepare an "aphrodisiac" buffet (chocolate, strawberries, whip cream)
3. Try a shower or bubble bath for two (Don't forget the scented candle and music)
4. Trade massages with oil
5. "Netflix and ice cream"
6. Try dessert in bed...
7. Take a day to flirt *all* day!

8. Play a "strip" game

9. Make the night all about him or her (Start with "your wish is my command")

10. Do a blind "taste test." See if they can guess the flavors (Don't forget the blindfold)

11. Look through your wedding photos and/or videos

12. Get a "rendezvous" room

13. Do something unexpected for your spouse

14. Go to a drive-in movie

15. Have an indoor picnic on the floor

16. Play with edible body paint

17. Leave a love note on the mirror for your spouse using a colored dry erase marker

18. Purchase new night wear for him and lingerie for her

19. Do something you did early in your marriage that you haven't done in a while

20. Spend a day doing whatever your spouse wants to do. Don't forget to take turns

21. Play tourist and visit a new part of your state/country

22. Go to your local orchard and pick seasonal fruit together

23. Have a cooking contest and see who cooks the best dish

24. Create a "Good for one free_____" (fill in the blank) voucher for your spouse

25. Order takeout just for dessert

26. Go to a virtual "live" concert on YouTube

27. Play "remember this" reminisce and take turns playing each other songs

28. Slow dance to your favorite love songs

29. Send spicy texts using only emojis throughout the day

30. Make your bedroom your favorite place in the house. Freshen it up to spice it up!

Remember, romance is simply "**R**ecognizing **O**pportunities and **M**aintaining **A**ffection **N**ecessary for **C**reating **E**verlasting love." Marriage does not have to be humdrum, where you are relegated to just remembering the good ol' days of romance when you were dating. As long as you have your spouse, every day has great potential. It's all about perspective. Everything worth having and keeping takes time and intentionality. You, your spouse, and your marriage are worth the effort.

YOUR STORY

We hope that you enjoyed this section, now the rest is up to you! In this section, we want you to create your own date night.

Review the lists provided above and write down romantic ideas you would like to try in order of interest.

1.

2.

3.

4.

5.

HOMEWORK CHALLENGE #8

Create Your Own Date Night

Create the following date nights listed below. Don't forget to be creative and add the dates to your calendar!

1. Home-Bound Date Idea: _____

Date_____

2. Home-Bound Date Idea: _____

Date_____

3. Home-Bound Date Idea: _____

Date_____

4. Home-Bound Date Idea: _____

Date_____

5. Home-Bound Date Idea: _____

Date_____

Did you complete the list and homework challenge?

If you did, then you and your spouse should reward yourselves with any of the above ideas.

We commit to rewarding ourselves by:

_____

We hope that revved things up! So, let's take a look under your marriage hood to learn a few D.I.Y (Do It Yourself) tips! We want to make sure you can optimize and maintain what you've learned for years to come.

Chapter Nine

Under the Hood with Bryan

*M*arriage, like any high-performance vehicle, requires regular maintenance to ensure longevity and optimal performance. Conducting preventative maintenance checks will allow you to get in front of issues that can cause potential problems down the road if left unchecked. Most times, you may not know there is a problem. If you hear or feel something is "off," you should not wait until the "check engine" light appears on your dashboard. Regular diagnostic tests can uncover issues that cannot be readily seen or heard and can quickly point to problem areas saving you time, money, and long repair times.

The foundation of any marriage relationship is love; however, you need a few more components to make the marriage run efficiently and successfully. Just like a car needs more than a sleek, fancy exterior body; it also needs an engine, fuel, ignition, exhaust, electrical, suspension, and braking systems. Much like these systems, love also has a system that makes a marriage run optimally. You must be able to understand how your love systems works, be able to identify and fix potential problems and reduce the likelihood of a breakdown in the future.

Love Systems

Let's start by checking under the hood and viewing some of the major love systems you should be aware of using the "Love Scripture" I Corinthians 13:4–7 as the foundation. We will cover the 12 basic love components and systems that keeps your marriage and loving relationship in proper running order. After you've familiarized yourself with the basic components, you will find a short comprehensive D.I.Y (Do It Yourself) list of items you should check regularly to ensure your marriage's optimum operating performance.

Love is patient; love is kind. It does not envy; it does not boast; it is not proud. It does not dishonor others; it is not self-seeking; it is not easily angered; it keeps no record of wrongs. Love does not delight in evil but rejoices with the truth. It always protects, always trusts, always hopes, always perseveres.

I Corinthians 13:4–7 (NIV)

#1 - Love Is Patient:
Power Steering Patience

No matter how proficient your driving skills are, you can't go very far without power steering. Power steering allows you to turn the tires with ease, and without it, your muscles would rival those of Hercules. Patience takes a certain amount of spiritual strength and can be pretty hard to navigate married life without it. Just like power steering fluid in your car helps maintain a smoother riding experience, patience keeps your relationship running smoothly. Patient love allows you to understand with ease that we won't always think, act, or respond the same way as our spouse would and that's ok because everyone is a work in progress.

Patience Systems Check

⊙ Think before you speak.

⊙ Take a break if you need to.

⊙ Gain clarity when you don't understand.

⊙ Don't assume the worst about your spouse.

⊙ Understand your triggers and what may be causing you to become impatient.

⊙ Always be mindful your spouse may not always see things the way you do.

#2 - Love Is Kind:
Keep It Kind Cooling system

There's nothing like a blast of cold air from the air conditioner on a hot, humid day. It sure makes the journey much more enjoyable and comfortable on a long road trip. Kindness is like that in many ways because it "conditions" the air, turning what could potentially be a heated argument into a cool, air-conditioned atmosphere making your home a sanctuary of peace and comfort. Kindness is always mindful of its words because it's not always what you say but how you say it. It causes conditions in the air of your marriage to be more pleasant, allowing you and your spouse to both be at ease. Set the right temperature in your marriage; you can be either a thermometer or a thermostat. A thermometer reflects the temperature of its environment and is influenced by the conditions in the room. A thermostatic does quite the opposite, it changes and regulates the temperature and mood of the room. Use kind and gentle words with your spouse and watch how, in minutes, it can turn a difficult situation around.

Kindness Systems Check

⊙ Ask your spouse, "What can I do for you today?"

⊙ Know your spouse's love language. Is it Words of Affirmation? Quality Time? Receiving Gifts? Acts of Service? or Physical Touch?

⊙ Be intentionally observant: Find something to compliment and appreciate about your spouse on a daily basis.

⊙ Start a random act of kindness challenge for a month with your spouse as the sole recipient.

#3 - Love Does Not Envy: Clean Envy Out of Your Engine

Envy desires what another person has or wishes the person did not possess it. In car terms, envy is like the nasty deposits of sludge formed within the engine, leading to reduced fuel economy, loss of horsepower, and engine failure. Envy slows one's own progress because it is too consumed or focused on another's life or success. Envy can take the form of competitiveness in a marriage relationship. It reveals itself when one spouse makes more money, receives an accolade the other did not, is more artistically talented, or has a more prestigious career. Each spouse contributes to the relationship in different ways, and they should both be recognized and appreciated. Most times we don't even realize this has happened because it can be very subtle. The good news is we don't have to stay that way. Understanding and appreciating your invaluable contribution to the relationship, in addition to supporting each other will restore your love, fuel economy, and horsepower. You can remove and dissolve any sludge buildup in your marriage by being each other's biggest supporters.

Generosity Systems Check

⊙ Value the skills and talents of your spouse; we are all born with different gifts and abilities.

⊙ Be happy and supportive of your spouse when they succeed. When they win, you both win.

⊙ Think of yourselves as a team; figure out ways you can maximize your gifts together to make your marriage, life, or business more successful.

⊙ Don't compare your marriage to that of another couple. Everyone has their own unique challenges. The grass always looks greener on the other side, but everyone has a few brown patches.

⊙ View each other as equal parts that contribute in different ways.

#4 - Love Does Not Boast: Muffle Your Boasting

Boasting is similar to a car without a muffler. A muffler "muffles" and filters the sound of toxic gasses leaving the engine, and it can be deafeningly loud without one. A boastful person is very much like a car without a muffler; you usually hear them before you see them. They are good at drawing attention to themselves and can be quite irritating to those around them because pride elevates itself while putting others down.

Inflated egos have no room in a loving marriage. Each spouse has the right to their own opinion and ideas, and no spouse's way is better than the other's. This line of thinking is the essence of pride. Disregarding and dismissing your spouse's feelings and input opens the door to resentment, pulling you further away, but a little humility goes a long way. Recognize the contribution your spouse brings to the marriage. After all, a rising tide lifts all boats.

Humility Systems Check

⊙ Give more credit to others.

⊙ Instead of drawing attention to yourself, praise your spouse in front of others. Be your spouse's wingman/wingwoman.

⊙ Show more interest in others if you are more prone to bragging about your accomplishments.

⊙ Recognize your personal achievements were not attained by your hard work alone, but by the grace of God.

#5 - Love Is Not Rude:
Filter Out Rudeness

Have you ever seen pictures of what tobacco smoke does to the lungs? We're pretty sure mechanics can show you pictures of dirty car filters that are just as scary. As a vital component of the air intake system, an air filter is essential because it allows the engine to 'breathe.' The air filter's job is to filter out dirt and other foreign particles in the air, preventing them from entering the system and possibly damaging the engine.

Behaving rudely contaminates the air of any relationship. The recipient of the rude behavior may not know why they are being treated with such disdain or how to clear the air if the behavior is ongoing. Being rude to our spouse conveys we do not value their feelings or the relationship because we tend not to be rude to those we hold in high regard. Rudeness should be addressed so that it does not escalate into further disrespect. Putting systems in place to clear the air and address rudeness will allow your relationship to flourish. There are steps that you can take to address rude behavior. If the behavior does not change after many attempts, boundaries should be in place to protect your heart and feelings. A boundary is an action you choose to take or refuse to take to end a damaging behavior and save the relationship.

Consideration Systems Check

⊙ Step 1 -Have a loving and calm discussion telling your spouse what behavior you desire to see changed and why it is vital for the relationship.

⊙ Step 2 -Have a more assertive conversation if the first attempt doesn't change. Be a bit more matter of fact with your request but not attacking. "This really needs to change; let's talk about how we can make this work."

⊙ Step 3 -Begin putting boundaries in place. "I love you, but I have decided to..." and follow through on the boundary <u>consistently</u>.

#6 - Love Is Not Self-Seeking: Wipe Away Self-Seeking

On any long journey driving thousands of miles, your car is sure to be battered by insects along the way. Depending on where you're traveling, especially if you're driving to the southern parts of the country in the United States, you can find your windshield blanketed with insects you've picked up along the way. There is nothing more frustrating than pressing your washer lever, and all you see are the remaining droplets of fluid being forced out of the spray nozzle while your wipers are scraping across your windshield with little to no fluid on them, making your bug problem even worse. All the while, diminishing your visibility, and preventing you from seeing the road clearly up ahead.

Being selfish and self-seeking is the inability to see how your behavior may affect the future of your relationship. In marriage, it's important to see ourselves and our spouse clearly. Self-seeking blinds and can steer your relationship off course, causing a life-altering event. Remember, you are a unit, and you *both* have needs, wants, and desires. Seek to gain a clearer perspective of the needs of your spouse.

Perspective Systems Check

⊙ Think of your marriage in terms of "we" rather than "I".

⊙ Take turns making decisions.

⊙ Collaborate and negotiate; look at ways you can both win.

⊙ When needs and preferences are different, put yourself in your spouse's shoes.

⊙ Ask yourself, "How would I feel if the shoe were on the other foot?" (i.e. concerns decisions being made, tone of voice, reaction)

#7 - Love Is Not Easily Angered: Cooler Heads Prevail; They Don't Radiate

Have you ever seen a car on the side of the road with steam pouring out from under the hood? Maybe it has even happened to you; it certainly has to us. Can you guess how this happened? There is a good chance it happened because the engine overheated due to a radiator issue. The radiator pulls heat away from your engine and protects your car from temperature-related problems. A car engine ideally runs between 180 and 210 degrees Fahrenheit, and if your car gets hotter than this, the engine will start to overheat.

We will inevitably have a discussion with our spouse that may leave us fuming, however, love is not easily angered, meaning it's not easily irritated, provoked, or annoyed. We should not be so overly sensitive or thin-skinned that we become overly aggressive or cause emotional injury to our spouse by the way we speak to them. When tempers rise and we feel like smoke is coming out of our ears, we shouldn't allow our anger to get the better of us causing us to make a temporary decision that may take a lifetime to repair. Cooler heads always prevail. Putting in cooling techniques will always prevent the argument from escalating. If you find you have been easily angered lately, give your anger to God, seek help to find out why, and find ways to manage it. In some cases, the anger could be the result of fear or fatigue.

Cooling Systems Check

⊙ Pray for strength and guidance.

⊙ Don't "hit below the belt" when disagreeing with your spouse.

⊙ Don't evade. State honestly and clearly why you are angry.

⊙ Ask yourself "Why am I really angry?" Are you afraid? Are you trying to defend or protect something that is important to you?

⊙ When disagreeing, stick to the subject at hand; be sure not to bring up past issues until you've resolved the current one.

#8 - Love Keeps No Record of Wrongs: Put the Brakes On

British author C.S. Lewis wrote, "Everyone says forgiveness is a lovely idea until they have to forgive someone." Doesn't it seem that our spouse should be the easiest person to forgive, but is sometimes the hardest as we hold on to old hurts and perceived wrongs?

It's very tempting to go past the point of no return when they have not met our expectations. Put the brakes on when you are tempted to criticize and keep a laundry list of things that your spouse did, didn't do, or you thought they should have done but failed to. If we ask for forgiveness, God says that He would forgive and would no longer remember our wrongs as far as the east is from the west; then why should we not want to do the same for your spouse?

Colossians 3:13–14 also says, "Forgive whatever grievances you may have against one another. Forgive as the Lord forgave you, and overall these virtues put on love, which binds them all together in perfect unity." Forgive and let the past be the past.

Brakes Systems Check

⊙ Once you've discussed the problem, make the needed adjustments, forgive, and let it go.
⊙ Tell your spouse how you feel and seek ways to resolve what's hurting you.
⊙ Negate the wrongs by keeping in your mind a list of all the *good* things about your spouse and dwell on those things.

#9 - Love Does Not Delight in Evil but Rejoices in the Truth: Focus on the Positive

Here's the scenario: You're stranded at the local grocery store with a dead battery, but thankfully you have a friend who's willing to get out of bed at 8:00 a.m. on a Saturday morning to bring you jumper cables. They don't plan to offer you AAA customer service, so they drop them off and head back to bed. But there's one problem, you don't know how to hook them up to the battery. You only remember there is a positive and a negative cable. Hopefully, you have your phone to find the answer on the internet. Getting your positive and negative charges mixed up on the battery terminal can cause a spark igniting hydrogen fumes from the battery, which can not only negatively impact your car but can be harmful to you as well.

Love does not delight in seeing other's fail, but rejoices in the truth. You can either be on the negative side of evil or the positive side of love. Being negative or delighting in evil can cause your marriage irreparable harm. We should always rejoice in the success of our spouse. When they accomplish something commendable such as passing an exam, graduating from school, or receiving a promotion, it should be celebrated. In contrast, if they fail at something, the last thing we'd want to do is "delight in evil," by being delighted in their failure or shortcomings. That certainly is not love.

Battery Systems Check

⊙ Make sure your spouse knows by your actions that you will always have their back.

⊙ Delight in the positive things your spouse is involved in.

⊙ Make a conscious effort to focus on and talk about positive things, not people, places, or things that are negative or evil.

⊙ Create an environment where your spouse always measures up in your eyes.

#10 - Love Always Protects: Cover Your Marriage

Though not technically "under the hood," every vehicle has a hood that serves to protect the performance components of the car, including all of the above-mentioned systems. The hood prevents the exposure of these vital parts from the elements of snow, rain, and sunlight. This is the hallmark of a good, healthy marriage relationship. The inner workings and challenges you face should be protected and remain between you, God, and your spouse, particularly during challenging seasons or disagreements. Love protects and covers.

Once you have forgiven a past offense or misunderstanding, you should not share the negative details of your marriage with your family or friends. Failure to protect your spouse can disrupt family dynamics for years. Telling your family about a hurtful disagreement can cause them to dislike your spouse long after you have both made up, forgiven, and even forgotten about the incident. Please understand, we are not proposing you cover up abuse of any kind mental, physical, emotional, or otherwise. If you find you are experiencing any of those issues, the appropriate assistance should be sought.

Love Protects Systems Check

⊙ Pray for your spouse daily.

⊙ Protect your spouse physically, emotionally, and mentally.

⊙ Don't speak negatively about your spouse to your family or friends. Remember, one day you will make up and you want your spouse's relationship with them to remain intact.

⊙ Don't take unnecessary risks with your family's future. (i.e., betting the farm, poor financial planning, and investments)

⊙ Protect your marriage from the scrutiny of others by not delving into sensitive information about your marriage.

#11 - Love Always Trusts: Transmit Trust

We have two different vehicles and both are pretty reliable. The first one we purchased in 2004 and the other in 2011. The first car looks great on the outside. It still has a new car shine and looks the same as the day we purchased it; however, we would never trust the transmission to take us on a 100 mile round-trip journey. The second vehicle is very reliable and could take us a bit farther. However, we save those long distance trips for our dream car, the Dodge Challenger, which happened to be the car we were driving in during our Mohave Desert mishap.

Although we do not trust our cars to travel long distances. Trust seeks to go the distance with the ones they love. Love in the form of trust is not cynical or suspicious; it looks to believe the best about others until it's proven otherwise. Trust is not gullible but seeks to see the one it loves in the best light. It takes into account everyone misses the mark, but has the potential to change. Trust has a consistent track record and must be dependable even after many years of saying, "I do." Based on our consistent actions, we want our spouse to know they can always depend on us in every season of marriage and will not lessen the effort we initially put into making the marriage work. Trust and intimacy grows over time. It is the greatest commodity you have with your spouse; if you lose it, you may never fully regain it. Protect it, because it is priceless.

Trust Systems Check

⊙ Give your spouse an opportunity to gain your trust.

⊙ Build trust gradually by staying true to your word.

- Always tell the truth even if you feel your spouse will be upset.

- Show you are trustworthy by keeping confidences.

- Trust your spouse by asking questions and believing they will make the right decision for your relationship and family.

#12 - Love Always Hopes and Perseveres

Is your marriage like the little blue train in the story *The Little Engine That Could*? This amazing story has encouraged both young and old for over a century. When faced with the challenge of pulling a much larger cargo train over a mountain that he'd never climbed, the little blue train faced what seemed to be an insurmountable task. He shares with the broken red train who sought assistance that he'd only experienced pulling switcher trains and had never gone over the mountain, but he was up for the challenge. The little red train hoped that he could help and did not consider the fact that he had never done it before. The story goes on to inspire us that although the little blue train charted into unfamiliar territory, he told himself a number of times " I think I can, I think I can," until he finally reached his goal, climbing to the top of the mountain.

Although this is a children's story, it reveals a timeless principle of hope, perseverance and belief. Marriage requires all of those things. Many marriages will go through seasons that they've never faced, but if both spouses are willing to hope, persevere and believe they can make it, they can successfully overcome any mountain that seems to be in their way. If you believe it will work, it will work; it all starts in the mind and the resolution to persevere. Don't be afraid of perseverance. It will only bring you closer, make your marriage stronger, and provide you with the endurance you'll both need for all of your adventures up ahead. You can get over any mountain together. If you think you can, you most certainly will.

Hope and Perseverance Systems Check

⊙ Trust God with your marriage.

⊙ Be flexible and understand there will be changes, pressures, and challenges that you can overcome when you work together.

⊙ Always remember you're in it together and use your strengths to get to your desired destination.

⊙ Think of all your marital successes and how you overcame them together.

YOUR STORY

You've had an opportunity to review the Love Systems and its basic components.

Out of the twelve systems noted, write down 3 systems you will check regularly.

Why are those systems important to your marriage?

1.) System:

_____

System Importance:

_____

2.) System:

_____

System Importance:

_____

3.) System:

_____

System Importance:

_____

HOMEWORK CHALLENGE #9

Systems Checks

We all need to ensure our marriage receives regular maintenance. Continue to check your love systems regularly to ensure your marriage's optimum operating performance.

1. Read and memorize I Corinthians 13:4–7

Love is patient; love is kind. It does not envy; it does not boast; it is not proud. It does not dishonor others; it is not self-seeking; it is not easily angered; it keeps no record of wrongs. Love does not delight in evil but rejoices with the truth. It always protects, always trusts, always hopes, always perseveres.

I Corinthians 13:4–7 (NIV)

---

2. Incorporate these love systems in your weekly/monthly temperature checks. Don't forget to schedule and add your time together on your calendar!

Did you complete the questions and homework challenge?

If you did, you know what to do, reward yourselves! Allow yourself some free time to do any activity you enjoy.

We commit to rewarding ourselves by:

Chapter Ten

12-Point Relationship Inspection Checklist

I n the previous chapter, you had an opportunity to take a comprehensive look at many of the major components and systems under your marriage hood that keep it in proper working order. This will now give you the ability to keep an eye out for any existing or potential problems that you can fix on the spot or as needed. Our goal is to provide you with the tools and information you need to keep your marriage running in tip-top shape because we are committed to seeing your marriage go the distance. Sometimes it can be pretty obvious when your marriage may not be performing as optimally as you would like.

Leaks, squeaks, and billows of smoke are indications that a bit of maintenance may be required. No problem, we have included a list of items you should check for throughout different times and seasons in your marriage. Some should be checked daily, monthly and others annually. When you identify an area where repairs are needed, refer back to your Marriage Maintenance

Service Manual in the previous chapter for additional guidance and instructions.

✓ **Romance Repairs**

- ⊙ Do you have a regular date night?
- ⊙ Have you told your spouse you love them today?
- ⊙ Did you show them appreciation today?
- ⊙ Have you scheduled time for romance?
- ⊙ Have you made time for physical and emotional intimacy?

✓ **Attitude Alignment**

- ⊙ Are you speaking to each other in a kind and respectful manner?
- ⊙ Are you exhibiting patience towards each other?
- ⊙ Have you been resentful towards your spouse?
- ⊙ Are you taking steps to be more open and readjust your perspective?

✓ **Sorry Services**

- ⊙ Do you need to apologize to your spouse?
- ⊙ Did you apologize when you discovered you were wrong?
- ⊙ Were you able to see the part you played when you disagreed?
- ⊙ Did you attempt to make things better after a misunderstanding?

✓ **Forgiveness Filters**

⊙ Do you need to forgive your spouse?

⊙ Are you holding anything against each other? If so, what?

⊙ Are you attempting to resolve any issues of unforgiveness?

⊙ Are you considering each of you have your own unique weaknesses?

⊙ Have you forgiven yourself?

⊙ Are you keeping a record of your spouse's wrongdoings?

✓ **Turbocharged Temperaments**

⊙ Are there times when you can be too controlling?

⊙ Are you actively working on solving disagreements?

⊙ Are you "giving in" to end the argument?

⊙ Are you concerned with winning? Resolving the issue?

⊙ Are you being stubborn in some areas?

⊙ Are you requiring everyone to do things your way?

GENERAL MAINTENACE SERVICES

✓ Love Language

- ⊙ Do you know your spouse's love language?

- ⊙ Do you know your spouse's apology language?

- ⊙ Do you know what makes your spouse feel valued and loved?

- ⊙ How are you fueling up your spouse's Love Bank and Trust Tank?

✓ Quality Communication

- ⊙ Can your spouse tell you how they feel?

- ⊙ Do you avoid dealing with issues when you are upset?

- ⊙ Can you share with your spouse your needs and wants?

- ⊙ How do you respond when your spouse shares his or her feelings?

✓ Supportive Styles

- ⊙ What have you done for your spouse lately?

- ⊙ When was the last time you asked, "Is there anything I can do for you?"

- ⊙ Did you share with your spouse how they can support you?

- ⊙ Are you listening to your spouse?

✓ **Love and Leisure**

⊙ What activities can you enjoy together?

⊙ Are there activities you are involved in that are interfering with your quality time together?

⊙ Are you balancing your time together?

⊙ Do you give your spouse time alone to do the things they enjoy to help them decompress?

✓ **Sexpectations**

⊙ What are your expectations when it comes to intimacy with your spouse?

⊙ Are you meeting and fulfilling each other's sexual needs? If not, why?

⊙ Are you comfortable sharing with your spouse your sexual needs, desires and expectations?

⊙ Are there issues that prevent you from having the sexual and non-sexual intimacy you desire to have with your spouse? Have you discussed it?

⊙ How are you working together to resolve any barriers to intimacy?

✓ **Family and Friends Day**

⊙ How do you manage your extended family's expectations?

⊙ Have you established boundaries with your family to protect your marriage?

⊙ Are you too involved in the affairs of your extended family? Adult Children?

⊙ What do you appreciate about your spouse's family? In-laws? Friends?

⊙ Are you attempting to bring cohesiveness to your blended family?

✓ Division of Labor

⊙ Are you balancing household responsibilities (Bills, Shopping, Cooking Cleaning, Childcare, etc.)?

⊙ Is there an imbalance in the household responsibilities?

⊙ What household chores does your spouse prefer to do?

⊙ Have you considered swapping chores? (Ex. one spouse cooks, the other cleans the kitchen. One spouse washes the laundry, while the other folds)

⊙ Are you keeping your end of the household chores and responsibility bargain?

Chapter Eleven

Marriage Takes Three

If one person falls, the other can reach out and help. But someone who falls alone is in real trouble. Likewise, two people lying close together can keep each other warm. But how can one be warm alone? A person standing alone can be attacked and defeated, but two can stand back-to-back and conquer. Three are even better, for a triple-braided cord is not easily broken.

Ecclesiastes 4:10–12 (NLT)

What's the Secret?

*W*e've been asked more times than we can count, "How do you make it work after twenty-one years of marriage?" "Do you really still like and love each other after all those years?" "What's the secret?" Our answer? Several significant events happened in our lives that created the strong bond that we have today. Every marriage has its own unique story and life events that bind them together. You just have to be willing to see the beauty in the process. We could easily say communication, humility, forgiveness, and acceptance are the secret, but having a good relationship that you desire to keep for a lifetime requires all of those things and more. We've been focusing on the journey throughout the book; however, you can't forget to pack a few provisions that will nourish you as well as satisfy your sweet tooth along the way; making the journey so much sweeter. So, we will share a few special sweet morsels with you.

We discovered love is the foundation of all marriages, but it's not the only thing that keeps and binds you together as a couple. We all have to build our very own unique Couple Cake and determine how sweet we want it to be. Marriage is much like taking a scenic journey together, but it is also very much like the cake on your wedding day. All of the ingredients came together so beautifully, but it did not start that way.

It takes time and skill, and let's not forget heat, to create something so beautiful and sweet that you both can enjoy. Both the essence of love and cake have a base. A cake isn't just flour; flour is the base, and many other ingredients must be added and mixed in to get the results you're looking for. You have to add in eggs, butter, sugar, vanilla extract, baking powder, and milk, to name just a few essential ingredients. Each of those ingredients eaten separately may not be the tastiest, but when you combine them all, and in the right hands, it can turn out to be quite the masterpiece. Couples sometimes look at their disagreements and misunderstandings as a single ingredient leaving a bad taste in their mouth, not understanding that when you put all of the ingredients together, the good times and the bad, you create your very own uniquely customized sweet masterpiece. There were years when we didn't understand this concept. We thought our life was a recipe for disaster, but as we began to see how things were working together, we saw triumph in tragedy and beauty in the ashes. So when a couple asks us what is the one thing that has kept us together, we share with them four of our secret ingredients.

Love & Tragedies

The first ingredient that binds us together were tragedies we had to endure. We learned how to persevere and stick together long enough to see the triumphs in the end. Throughout our marriage, there were a number of tragedies that we had to press through and found we had to bandage one another up while also having to tend to our own private personal wounds.

We went through and survived: financial ruin, miscarriages, fertility issues; learning we'd never be able to have our own natural children, the death of two parents, the loss of three jobs, betrayals by those we loved, tens of thousands of dollars were stolen from us, utility disconnections forced us to stay in a hotel, the threat of homelessness plagued us, we received food from food banks, and financial assistance from family and friends, we faced depression, dire health conditions and much more. We could have thrown in the towel after the first five events, but we held on to hope during those times when the situation seemed absolutely hopeless, being encouraged by scriptures:

And we know that in all things God works for the good of those who love him, who have been called according to his purpose.

Romans 8:28 (NIV)

Now thanks be unto God, who always causeth us to triumph in Christ and who maketh manifest through us the savor of His knowledge in every place.

2 Corinthians 2:14 (KJV)

We persevered, drew closer to God, each other, and built a lasting friendship, camaraderie, and an unbreakable bond. We eventually came out on the other side strengthened in our love because we persevered.

Love & Triumph

The second ingredient is always keeping our hearts full of hope, understanding that things can be worse but will always get better. We cherish and appreciate the good times while we have them and celebrate our triumphs. We found working together and supporting others made our life more rewarding because we realize there are people who are much less fortunate than we are.

As the years progressed and we began to walk out of what seemed like constant battles, many doors began to open for us. We were blessed to mentor hundreds of young people and children in our city and across the country. Our finances were restored; we are able to give more than we ever expected to. We are spiritual parents to three amazing children, Maurcell,

Mia, and Jania. We've also had opportunities to travel, help the poor, support orphanages, build houses, churches, and hospitals in Romania and Guatemala. We are conference speakers, world travelers, mentor couples to help mend broken marriages and relationships, and because of it, we have grown rich in faith, hope, and love.

Love & Prayer

The third ingredient we use was a gift we received on our wedding day. Our pastor David C. Rourk married us and prayed a prayer of blessing over us that carries us to this very day. We didn't understand it at the time, but we believe this has been the foundation of our marriage. He prayed that God would quickly bring us back to love if we ever found ourselves drifting apart. We thought it a bit odd at the time and didn't understand it until many years later. That blessing and those words were made manifest in our lives throughout the years. We always find ourselves being drawn back together after times of disagreement and miscommunication, desiring to reconnect and reestablish our friendship.

This is also our prayer for you as you read this love manual. We extend that same blessing to you today and pray that nothing and no one comes in between you and your spouse to cause your love to grow cold. We pray that you'll both keep a candle lit, so that you'll always be able to find your way back to each other and out of the darkest places.

Our Three-Fold Cord

Through it all, God is at the center of our marriage. He is the most important secret ingredient in our Couple Cake because He is the one that brings it all together so beautifully. The love of God helped us to love each other during the times when we weren't always so loveable. We make a habit of placing little trinkets and tchotchke's in our home to remind ourselves of our friendship and love. There is a beautiful poem on a plaque that we received on our wedding day that hangs outside of our bedroom door. We walk past it many times a day, and it reminds us daily we are not in this marriage alone; there is a God who has shown us the true meaning of love. The plaque entitled Marriage Take Three by Beth Stuckwisch has blessed our marriage immensely.

Your marriage is a beacon of hope to the world. You are not just fighting for your own happiness; you are fighting for the legacy of those who will come after you. Marriage is much more than a ceremony where you get to dress up for a day. It is a covenant between two people that are committed to the journey. This covenant is a beautiful example of Christ's love for his people. Letting the world know that true love does exist, it can stand staunchly in the face of storms, and it can endure. By this example of love, you can show others:

- You can disagree and forgive
- You can be faithful to your spouse
- You can freely love and receive love
- You can have a healthy family structure

- You can have a loving and fulfilling relationship
- You can go through storms together and come out stronger

We have given you a bird's eye view into our journey, and we hope that you and your spouse will create lasting memories for many years to come. May you have the journey of a lifetime, not forgetting to stop, rest, laugh, and love.

Chapter Twelve

Holy Horsepower!

*M*arriage can be challenging and it can be difficult to share with others what you are going through, but God always has a listening ear. Friends can be a great support, but we should always turn to the one who created marriage, God. As Christians, we believe scriptures in the bible have the ability to breathe life back into any situation that feels irretrievably broken; our hearts, relationships, friendships, and even our marriage. It did for us.

Not only does Jesus heal broken hearts, but He also gives great joy and hope in abundance. No matter what's happened in the past, is currently happening in the present, or what may happen in the future, God loves you. One of our favorite scriptures is Isaiah 49:16 *"See; I have engraved you on the palm of my hands; your walls are ever before me."* God is so cool and loves you so much, He has a tattoo of you, and He never misses a beat concerning anything that's important to you. He said He even knows the number of hairs on your head! (Luke 12:7) That's how much He loves you and is aware of every little detail concerning you. So no matter how you feel, happy, sad, angry, lonely, or finding it challenging to forgive, He is there to listen and to help you. You can do that by reading His love letter to you, the Bible.

Use these scriptures verses to add a bit of horsepower to your prayer life and marriage. As you read, meditate on them, speak them out, believe them, and pray them over your spouse and family. They will encourage you and have the ability to transform your heart, mind, and life.

We have categorized them based on general topics and seasons you may be experiencing individually or as a couple. So use them as a means to encourage, build, and strengthen yourself spiritually, mentally, and emotionally.

Love

Love is the foundation of marriage. God is Love and gives us the ability to love during challenging times. Fill your spouse's love tank with the fuel of love and see how far you go.

o   And so we know and rely on the love God has for us. God is love. Whoever lives in love lives in God, and God in them.

1 John 4:16 (NIV)

o   Many waters cannot quench love; rivers cannot sweep it away. If one were to give all the wealth of one's house for love, it would be utterly scorned.

Song of Songs 8:7 (NIV)

o   There are three things that are too amazing for me, four that I do not understand; the way of an eagle in the sky, the way of a snake on a rock, the way of a ship on the high seas, and the way of a man with a young woman.

Proverbs 30:18-19 (NIV)

o   My beloved is mine and I am his.

Song of Solomon 2:16 (NIV)

o   You have stolen my heart, my sister, my bride; you have stolen my heart with one glance of your eyes, with one jewel of your necklace.

Song of Songs 4:9 (NIV)

o How handsome you are, my beloved! Oh, how charming!

Song of Songs 1:16 (NIV)

o How delightful is your love, my sister, my bride! How much more pleasing is your love than wine, and the fragrance of your perfume more than any spice!

Song of Songs 4:10 (NIV)

o Let him kiss me with the kisses of his mouth for your love is more delightful than wine.

Song of Songs 1:2 (NIV)

Husbands and Wives

Husbands and wives have a unique and spiritual bond they do not share with parents, children, family, or friends. Two unique people with different personalities, experiences, and family upbringing uniting to build a life together is a mystery of oneness. As you establish boundaries in your marriage, you can protect the union and create an unbreakable bond that can withstand the test of time.

○ So God created mankind in his own image, in the image of God he created them; male and female he created them. God blessed them and said to them, be fruitful and increase in number; fill the earth and subdue it. Rule over the fish in the sea and the birds in the sky and over every living creature that moves on the ground.

Genesis 1:27-28 (NIV)

○ Husbands, love your wives, just as Christ loved the church and gave himself up for her to make her holy, cleansing her by the washing with water through the word and to present her to himself as a radiant church, without stain or wrinkle or any other blemish, but holy and blameless. In this same way, husbands ought to love their wives as their own bodies. He who loves his wife loves himself. After all, no one ever hated their own body, but they feed and care for their body, just as Christ does the church for we are members of his body.

Ephesians 5:25-30 (NIV)

o   Be completely humble and gentle; be patient, bearing with one another in love. Make every effort to keep the unity of the Spirit through the bond of peace.

Ephesians 4:2-3 (NIV)

o   Be devoted to one another in love. Honor one another above yourselves.

Romans 12:10 (NIV)

o   Therefore, what God has joined together, let no one separate.

Mark 10:9 (NIV)

o   Two are better than one, because they have a good return for their labor

Ecclesiastes 4:9 (NIV)

o   The man who finds a wife finds a treasure and he receives favor from the LORD

Proverbs 18:22 (NLT)

Forgiveness

Over time repeated hurts and disappointments can chip away at that love you have for your spouse. Forgiveness and repentance (turning away from things that hurt your spouse, not just being sorry) can reestablish your connection with each other. There will be times of disappointments but working toward forgiveness is always the goal. Remove the barriers that attempt to keep you from forgiving, know God desires for us to forgive one another.

o Therefore, as God's chosen people, holy and dearly loved, clothe yourselves with compassion, kindness, humility, gentleness and patience. Bear with each other and forgive one another if any of you has a grievance against someone. Forgive as the Lord forgave you. And over all these virtues put on love, which binds them all together in perfect unity.

Colossians 3:12-14 (NIV)

o Whoever would foster love covers over an offense, but whoever repeats the matter separates close friends.

Proverbs 17:9 (NIV)

o Get rid of all bitterness, rage and anger, brawling and slander, along with every form of malice. Be kind and compassionate to one another, forgiving each other, just as in Christ God forgave you.

Ephesians 4:31-32 (NIV)

o Be merciful, just as your Father is merciful. Do not judge, and you will not be judged. Do not condemn, and you will not be condemned. Forgive, and you will be forgiven.

Luke 6:36-37 (NIV)

o For if you forgive other people when they sin against you, your heavenly Father will also forgive you. But if you do not forgive others their sins, your Father will not forgive your sins.

Matthew 6:14-15 (NIV)

o Do not say, I'll do to them as they have done to me; I'll pay them back for what they did.

Proverbs 24:29 (NIV)

Anger

Anger is an emotion that lets us know that something is not working and must be corrected. However, we do not want to live in those feelings. Find out why you are angry. Is it because you want control, to get your way, were wronged, or attempting to find justice? Do not let anger control you; it can lead to even greater conflict, separate us from those closest to us, and even affect our health; combat anger with peace.

o My dear brothers and sisters, take note of this: Everyone should be quick to listen, slow to speak and slow to become angry.

James 1:19 (NIV)

o In your anger do not sin. Do not let the sun go down while you are still angry.

Ephesians 4:26 (NIV)

o Do to others as you would have them do to you.

Luke 6:31 (NIV)

o Don't sin by letting anger control you. Think about it overnight and remain silent.

Psalm 4:4 (NLT)

o But now you must also rid yourselves of all such things as these: anger, rage, malice, slander, and filthy language from your lips.

Colossians 3:8 (NIV)

o Stop being angry! Turn from your rage! Do not lose your temper it only leads to harm.

Psalm 37:8 (NLT)

o Whoever is patient has great understanding but one who is quick-tempered displays folly.

Proverbs 14:29 (NIV)

o A hot-tempered person stirs up conflict, but the one who is patient calms a quarrel.

Proverbs 15:18 (NIV)

o A person's wisdom yields patience; it is to one's glory to overlook an offense.

Proverbs 19:11 (NIV)

Your Words

What we say to our spouse can bless or damage our relationships. Words can bring life or bring death. What are you saying to your spouse? Are you encouraging or criticizing? Building up or tearing down? We eat the fruit of the words we sow. Sow grace, kindness, and love so that you can reap it back in abundance.

o   The tongue has the power of life and death, and those who love it will eat its fruit.

   Proverbs 18:21 (NIV)

o   The words of the reckless pierce like swords, but the tongue of the wise brings healing.

   Proverbs 12:18 (NIV)

o   Set a guard over my mouth, Lord; keep watch over the door of my lips.

   Psalm 141:3 (NIV)

o   A brother who has been insulted is harder to win back than a walled city, and arguments separate people like the barred gates of a palace.

   Proverbs 18:19 (NIV)

o   Those who guard their lips preserve their lives, but those who speak rashly will come to ruin.

   Proverbs 13:3 (NIV)

o   A gentle answer turns away wrath, but a harsh word stirs up anger.

Proverbs 15:1 (NIV)

o   If you claim to be religious but don't control your tongue, you are fooling yourself, and your religion is worthless.

James 1:26 (NLT)

o   If you want to enjoy life and see many happy days, keep your tongue from speaking evil and your lips from telling lies.

1 Peter 3:10 (NLT)

o   Let your speech always be gracious, seasoned with salt, so that you may know how you ought to answer each person.

Colossians 4:6 (NIV)

o   To answer before listening that is folly and shame.

Proverbs 18:13 (NLT)

Sexual Intimacy

Sexual intimacy celebrates the union you have with your spouse and brings you closer to together. God created sex, and not only that, he wants us to enjoy it. Make time for intimacy and enjoy the body of your spouse. Work to remove barriers that would try to rob you both of this beautiful God-given gift.

o   May your fountain be blessed, and may you rejoice in the wife of your youth. A loving doe, a graceful deer may her breasts satisfy you always, may you ever be intoxicated with her love.

Proverbs 15:15-17 (NLT)

o   His left arm is under my head, and his right arm embraces me.

Song of Solomon 2:6 (NLT)

o   Drink water from your own cistern, running water from your own well. Should your springs overflow in the streets, your streams of water in the public squares? Let them be yours alone, never to be shared with strangers.

Proverbs 15:15-17 (NLT)

o   Marriage should be honored by all, and the marriage bed kept pure

Hebrews 13:4 (NIV)

o   But because there is so much sexual immorality, each man should have his own wife, and each woman should have her own husband. The husband should fulfill his wife's sexual needs, and the wife should fulfill her husband's needs. The wife gives authority over her body to her husband, and the husband gives authority over his body to his wife.

1 Corinthians 7:2-4 (NIV)

o   Do not deprive each other of sexual relations, unless you both agree to refrain from sexual intimacy for a limited time so you can give yourselves more completely to prayer. Afterward, you should come together again so that Satan won't be able to tempt you because of your lack of self-control.

1 Corinthians 7:5 (NLT)

When You're Feeling Lonely

Sometimes we can feel misunderstood, possibly unloved, and alone during different seasons in marriage.

However, know you are loved and never alone because God has promised to never leave you or forsake you. When you begin feeling lonely read the scriptures below and make the extra effort to visit people, places, and things that celebrate you or things that bring you joy.

o   He heals the brokenhearted and binds up their wounds.

Psalm 147:3 (NIV)

o   In my distress I called to the LORD; I cried to my God for help. From his temple he heard my voice; my cry came before him, into his ears

Psalm 18:6 (NIV)

o   May your unfailing love be my comfort, according to your promise to your servant.

Psalm 119:76 (NIV)

o   Don't be afraid, for I am with you. Don't be discouraged, for I am your God I will strengthen you and help you. I will hold you up with my victorious right hand

Isaiah 41:10 (NLT)

o   Do not be afraid, for I have ransomed you. I have called you by name; you are mine. When you go through deep waters, I will be with you. When you go through rivers of difficulty, you will not drown.   When you walk through the fire of oppression, you will not be burned up; the flames will not consume you. For I am the LORD, your God, the Holy One of Israel, your Savior.

Isaiah 43:1-2 (NLT)

o   For your Creator will be your husband; the LORD of Heaven's Armies is his name! He is your Redeemer, the Holy One of Israel, the God of all the earth. For the LORD has called you back from your grief as though you were a young wife abandoned by her husband," says your God.

Isaiah 54:5-6 (NLT)

o   And I am convinced that nothing can ever separate us from God's love. Neither death nor life, neither angels nor demons, neither our fears for today nor our worries about tomorrow—not even the powers of hell can separate us from God's love. No power in the sky above or in the earth below—indeed, nothing in all creation will ever be able to separate us from the love of God that is revealed in Christ Jesus our Lord.

Roman 8:38-39 (NLT)

o   Come close to God and He will come close to you

James 4:8 (NLT)

ACKNOWLEGEMENTS

We'd like to first begin by thanking our amazing parents Satchtral Pitts Sr., Lawanza Lane, Dwight and Sheryl Covington. You have always been our biggest cheerleaders, and we could fill another book with pages of appreciation for all you've done for us. You have been such incredible role models, and we wouldn't be in this place in our lives without your love and support. We love, honor, and appreciate you more than the English language can express.

To our parents in heaven, Anna Leslie and Larry Owens Sr. we know you would be so proud of us, and although you are not here with us on earth, your love resides in our hearts.

We are eternally grateful for our spiritual father and mother, Pastor David Valle Sr. and Pastora Jeanette Valle. You saw us through many struggles and whisked us away during a time when we needed it the most. You dried our tears, strengthened us, and walked with us through the most challenging season of our marriage. Thank you so much for being there, helping us come out on the other end and engrafting us into your family.

Writing a book is challenging, and you need special people you can call on day or night with your crazy ideas and for reassurance. Siblings are tailor-made for such occasions. Many thanks to our siblings: Tanysha Pitts, Samara Lane-Black, Keith Owens, Satch Jr., and Sonia Pitts. We bugged you incessantly to read chapters, share your honest opinions, and lend your listening ear when as talked them off incessantly because of our excitement! You did it all, and we couldn't have done it without your love, encouragement, and support.

Tamara Parsons-Porter, you are an angel and a God-send. You read the very first page and redraft after redraft, not only are you my sister but my best friend. Thank you for providing us with your keen eye and creative suggestions. You encouraged us until we saw the finish line and helped us cross it. You are such an amazing person and we love you so much!

To Brian & Lisa Binion, and Laura & Paul Masterson, our very best friends, you have been with us from our first date to our wedding day. Thank you for your prayers and encouragement; we are so honored to call you our friends.

There is certainly no "I" in team. We were blessed with a team of talented, smart, honest, loving, and dedicated beta team members: Terrell and Felisha Brady, Ryland and Jerralyn Stephens, Toby and Kris Butler, Danielle Roque, Charnissa Scott-Seigler, Karen Bell-Moore, Pam Cowans, Beverly Davis, Michelle Lopez, Dr. Mary Bisbee-Burrows, and Pastor Dr. Barbara JP Thomas. Thank you for going over and beyond the call of duty. You are helping us strengthen marriages, relationships, and families nationally and internationally.

David and Alisa Curry, you are such an inspirational couple. Your excitement ignited our excitement even more when you committed to reading the book during your vacation in its rawest form. Your feedback was encouraging and helped us keep our eyes on the goal. We appreciate your love and support more than you'll ever know.

To Pastor Lonnel Brinson Sr., you saw the book finished before the first page was ever written. Thank you for your encouragement, prayers, and leadership. You are a true leader of leaders.

We want to extend a very special thank you to the Rourk and Bruce family. Thank you so much for welcoming us into your family. Your parents made our lives so much richer because of their model of love. The love they have for each other will live on for generations to come. Thank you for allowing us to adopt your parents and make them our own. We send our love and gratitude to Cheryl Rourk-Brown, Sonya Rourk-Miller, Karen Fletcher, Pastor Chris Rourk, Michael Bruce, Sonya Bruce, Gwendolyn Burroughs, Dwane Bruce, and Kimberly Armstrong. We love, honor, and thank you.

REFERENCES

Preface
Brela Delahoussaye, the founder of Romance Me https://www.loveofromance.com

Chapter 1
1. Harvard Medical School, *Love and The Brain*
https://neuro.hms.harvard.edu/harvard-mahoney-neuroscience-institute/brain-newsletter/and-brain/love-and-brain

Chapter 2
1. Gary D. Chapman, *Now You're Speaking My Language* (Tennessee: B&H Publishing, 2014)
2. Benson, K. (2017, October 4) *The Magic Relationship Ratio, according to science* (Retrieved from https://www.gottman.com/blog/the-magic-relationship-ratio-according-science/)

Chapter 3
1. DISC Profile, William Moulton Marston, *History of DISC*, (Retrieved from *https://www.discprofile.com/what-is-disc/history-of-disc*)

Chapter 5
1. Alexander Pope, *An Essay On Criticism* (Retrieved from https://www.poetryfoundation.org/articles/69379/an-essay-on-criticism)

Chapter 8
1. Gregory Berns, Ph.D., *Iconoclast: A Neuroscientist Reveals How to Think Differently* (Massachusetts: Harvard Business Review Press March 17, 2010)

BEFORE YOU GO

Thank you for Reading Marriage Maintenance: Getting Back On the Road To Romance. If you enjoyed this book, please consider leaving a review on Amazon. Your comments will help strengthen other married couples, especially newlyweds, who are trying to decide if this book will add value to their marriage.

We love working with couples and helping organizations establish communities that connect individuals together. If you are interested in forming small groups for couples, premarital classes, or would like to schedule the Littles for trainings or other speaking engagements, please contact us at:

Email: contact@tamlittle.com

Website: tamlittle.com

We would love to hear from you!

Bryan & Tam Little

Made in the USA
Coppell, TX
09 August 2021

60184869R00115